WHAT OTHERS ARE SAYING ABOUT 231 WAYS TO SAY I LOVE YOU

I JUST COMPLETED reading the newest publication by Robert W Lucas and I highly recommend it. It is good for couples dating, newlyweds, and those celebrating 30, 40, 50 and 60 years married. The message is loud and clear—COMMUNICATION. What is great about this resource is you can use it, share it, make your own list of your ways to get to know your partner better and to make love a priority again. I enjoy the friendship of many octogenarians and even when communication in the traditional sense is difficult or impossible because of hearing deficiency, lack of sight or diminished mind, they still communicate with the touch of a hand, a stroke of a hand on his/her face or a gentle kiss—they're saying, "I'm still here, I still love you." Well done Robert, another effective and thought provoking publication!

Barbara Tanzer, Co-Founder TBS Travel
www.OurCruiseAgent.com

THIS BOOK WORKS well for all ages. I've been married 57 years and I found new strategies to make our lives together more memorable. There are so many unique ideas that are easy to implement. It is obvious the author has common sense flavored by his experiences and creativity. Consider this book as a gift for your next bridal shower, a surprise for a good friend and most of all as a resource to expand your personal relationship with your loved one.

Sylvia Foy, Retired Human Resource Executive

LOVE IS ONE of the great emotions of humanity. Unfortunately, the challenges of daily life can erode the deep feelings and hope that only love can bring. Bob's book provides simple yet powerful ways of keeping your love of life, of your partner, of your friends fresh and alive. I recommend them all—and so will you!

Lou Coenen

For additional printed copies or bulk discounts use the ***Order Form*** at end of this book or contact:

Robert W. Lucas Enterprises
PO Box 180487
Casselberry, FL 32718-0487 USA

407-695-5535

http://www.robertwlucas.com

Pricing can be found on the order form at the end of this book.

231 Ways to Say *I Love You*

...and mean it

Robert W. Lucas

Success Skills Press

Published by Success Skills Press
Casselberry, Florida 32707 USA

Copyright © 2016 by Robert W. Lucas. All rights reserved.

Except as permitted under the United States Copyright Law of 1976, no part of this publication may be reproduced or distributed in any form or by any means, electronic or mechanical, including photocopying, recording or otherwise, or stored in a database or retrieval system, without the prior written permission of the copyright owner.

The content of this book contains the sole opinions of the author based on his experience and knowledge as a published author, along with references to others, and should be treated as such. All attempts have been made to ensure that all information, websites, and references contained in this book are correct and accurate at the time of publication. The content is provided for informational purposes. Neither the author nor the publisher make any warranties or representations related to content, nor do they assume any liability for errors, omissions, or inaccuracies of subject matter contained herein or for damages suffered as a result of content application. Any incorrect attributions in the book are inadvertent and will be corrected in future editions if notifications are made to the publisher.

This publication is designed to provide accurate and authoritative information in regard to the subject matter covered. It is sold with the understanding that neither the author nor the publisher is engaged in rendering legal, accounting, securities trading, or other professional services. If legal advice or other expert assistance is required, the services of a competent professional person should be sought.

Extracted from a Declaration of Principles Jointly Adopted by a Committee of the American Bar Association and a Committee of Publishers and Associations.

Editorial: Barbara Tanzer; Sharon Massen

Cover design by Joleene Naylor

Cover images courtesy of galdzer, Elenathewise, ifong, and canstockphoto

Book layout by DocUmeantDesigns.com

Heart clipart courtesy of https://openclipart.org

Distributed by Robert W. Lucas Enterprises

Printed in the United States of America.

Library of Congress Control Number: 2015914845

ISBN-10: 1939884012
ISBN-13: 978-1-939884-01-5

DEDICATION

DEDICATED TO MY father- and mother-in-law, Bob and Betty Wolfe, whose marriage and love for almost seven decades is a daily inspiration to their family and everyone else who knows him and her. The care and kindness that they share with one another encapsulates a relationship far stronger than the average couple could hope for in a lifetime.

Special thanks and appreciation to M.J. (*M*y *J*oy)—my wife, best friend, lover and life partner, who makes life meaningful and gives me purpose, drive and a reason to look forward to the new memories of tomorrow that we will make together.

Also dedicated to my children, Michael, Brittney and Todd in hopes that they realize the importance of having and holding onto the ones they love and continually striving to enhance their relationships.

Special thanks to the following friends, family members and colleagues for their support, encouragement and suggestions that made this book a reality:

Ryan Brown	Lenn Millbower
Sherry Coenen Brown	Joleene Naylor
Lou Coenen	Linda Sullivan
Sylvia Foy	Barbara Tanzer
Jennifer Harper	Steve Tanzer
Mark Massen	Bob Wolfe
Sharon Massen	Betty Wolfe
Zenee' Miller	Rex Wolfe

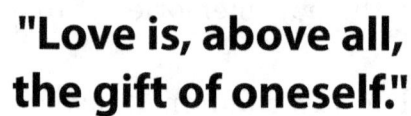

"Love is, above all,
the gift of oneself."

Jean Anouilh

WHY I LOVE YOU: Praise for My Wife

 From the day I first saw you I knew that you were different.

THERE ARE MANY things that I love about you. Many of which I have trouble putting into words.

The way you view the world intrigues me as you challenge me to look at daily events through your eyes.

The look in your eyes enchants me as I strive to better understand how someone as wonderful as you came to be in my life.

Your movements excite me and make me want to be near to you at all times.

The special qualities that you bring to our relationship and the world inspire me. Among these are your compassion, optimism, enthusiasm for life, and the ability to make me want to partner with you as we explore the riches of life and love together.

Most of all, I love the little things that you do that adds richness and joy to my life. This includes the ways in which you show that you believe in me and us through your love, touches, caring and continuing efforts to help our relationship grow and flourish.

I suppose the essence of why I love you is because you make me feel whole. You are the depth of my heart and my soul mate. I look forward to seeing you the first thing in the morning, when I return home after an absence and the last thing before I close my eyes to sleep.

I love you because you are special and because you are ***My Joy!***

CONTENTS

DEDICATION v

WHY I LOVE YOU: Praise for My Wife vii

PREFACE xxi

INTRODUCTION xxv

INTENSIFY YOUR RELATIONSHIP. 1

  #1   Work to Build Trust 1

  #2   Show Respect. 3

  #3   Accept Responsibility 6

  #4   Respect Privacy. 7

  #5   Be a Positive Role Model 8

  #6   Create a Couple's "To Do" List. 8

  #7   Read Relationship "How To" Books 8

  #8   Overlook Your Pet Peeves 9

  #9   Praise Your Loved One. 9

  #10 Don't Always Be Right 10

  #11 Let Your Loved One Choose a Movie 10

  #12 Let Your Emotional Guard Down 10

  #13 Attend Family Functions 10

  #14 Take Your In-Laws to Lunch 11

  #15 Give a "Thank You" Card 11

  #16 Don't Unload Your Frustrations 12

#17	Acknowledge Your Mistakes	12
#18	Remove the Television	12
#19	Start a Tradition	13
#20	Kiss and Make Up	13
#21	Remember That You Are Partners	14
#22	Commit to Improvement	14

BRING BACK THE ROMANCE 15

#23	Become a Committed Romantic	15
#24	Make a List of Things You Like	15
#25	Use Heart Shaped Ice Cubes	16
#26	Leave a Personal Recorded Message	16
#27	Print and Frame a Noted Poem	16
#28	Write a Love Poem or Song	17
#29	Sprinkle Rose Petals Over the Bed	17
#30	Send a Telegram	18
#31	Download Music of Love	18
#32	Put Your Initials in Concrete	18
#33	Post Your Message of Love	19
#34	Create a Special Award	19
#35	Write Your Own Wedding Vows	20
#36	Give Your Loved One a Sign	20
#37	Get a Tattoo	20
#38	Write I Love You in the Sand	21
#39	Share Your Love with the World	21
#40	Recreate Your First Date	21

#41	Write Love Messages in the Snow 21
#42	Buy a Boutonnière and Corsage. 22
#43	Play Hooky on Valentine's Day or Anniversary. 22
#44	Get Regular Formal Portraits Made 22
#45	Order Customized License Plates 23
#46	Rent a Beach Bungalow 23
#47	Have a Bumper Sticker Made 23
#48	Renew Your Wedding Vows 23
#49	Send a Series of Greeting Cards 24
#50	Cuddle While Watching Television 24
#51	Place the Winning Bid at an Auction. 25
#52	Keep a Relationship Scrapbook 25
#53	Purchase Customized Coffee Mugs 25
#54	Say "Goodnight" and "I Love You" 26
#55	Buy Flannel Sheets. 26

TAP THE ELEMENT OF SURPRISE 27

#56	Splurge for Front Row Seats 27
#57	Give a Calendar as a Present. 27
#58	Do Something Nice 28
#59	Treat to a Round of Golf. 28
#60	Send a Singing Mylar Balloon 28
#61	Surprise with a Special Treat 28
#62	Declare a Special Day. 29
#63	Pack a Special Surprise 29
#64	Surprise the Traveler 30

#65	Get Up Early and Go for Pastries	30
#66	Hide Messages of Love in Easter Eggs	31
#67	Put an Advertisement in the Newspaper	31
#68	Hire a High School Band or Choir	31
#69	Send Letters or Postcards	32
#70	Plan a Surprise Airport Greeting	32
#71	Rent a Billboard	33
#72	Prepare a Surprise Greeting	33
#73	Send a Congratulatory Card	34
#74	Send a Singing Telegram	34
#75	Have a Special Valentine's Day	34
#76	Create a Photo Screen Image	35
#77	Create a Video of Love	35
#78	Occasionally Hide Love Notes	36
#79	Record a Personal Message	36
#80	Call to Sing on Special Occasions	36
#81	Bake Customized Fortune Cookies	37
#82	Program a Custom Desktop Background Image	37
#83	Hide a Piece of Jewelry	37
#84	Plaster the House with Love Notes	38
#85	Write "I Love You" on a Piece of Fruit	39
#86	Place a Gift on the Pillow	39
#87	Celebrate with a Cupcake	39
#88	Have Flowers Delivered	39
#89	Prepare a Special Homecoming	40

#90	Hire a Limousine	40
#91	Put a Note in a Balloon	40
#92	Mail a Giant Greeting Card	41
#93	Throw a Surprise Party	41
#94	Hide a Love Letter	41

STRENGTHEN THE COMMUNICATION FLOW 43

#95	Be Considerate of Your Loved One	43
#96	Celebrate Your Love	43
#97	Attend Communication Classes	44
#98	Never Go To Bed Angry	44
#99	Start a Nightly Tradition	45
#100	Call to Say I Love You	46
#101	Use the Word "Please" in Requests	46
#102	Say the Words "I Love You"	46
#103	Write a Love Letter	47
#104	Discuss Daily Events	48
#105	Create a Secret Nonverbal Message	48
#106	Communicate Openly	49
#107	Call When You Are Going to Be Late	49
#108	Communicate During Sex	50
#109	Prepare a Relationship Questionnaire	50
#110	Establish a (VoIP) Account	51
#111	Acknowledge When You Are Wrong	51

RECAPTURE PASSION AND SENSUALITY.... 53

#112 Use Love Touches 53

#113 Play Strip Poker or Other Card Game.... 54

#114 Plan Regular Date Nights 54

#115 Watch Romantic, Sensual Movies 55

#116 Let Your Loved One Orchestrate Sex 55

#117 Make Love in Front of a Fireplace....... 55

#118 Fall Asleep Spooning 55

#119 Be Uninhibited Around Your Partner 56

#120 Share our Inner Feelings and Fantasies .. 56

#121 Use Passionate Kisses Freely............ 56

#122 Be Spontaneously Intimate 57

#123 Have Phone Sex 57

#124 Prepare a "Love String" 57

#125 Take a Bubble Bath or Shower Together . 58

#126 Take an Idea Excursion 58

#127 Spin for Sex........................... 59

#128 Plan an Intimate Evening 59

#129 Request a Play Date 59

REINFORCE CARING AND SECURITY......... 61

#130 Remember Special Dates 61

#131 Plan for a Financial Crisis 61

#132 Demonstrate Your Love in Small Ways... 63

#133 Sign Up for a Road Service Membership.. 64

#134 Sign Up for a CPR Class Together....... 64

#135 Kiss Your Loved One's Hand 65

#136 Allow Your Partner to Choose a Seat 65

#137 Bring Flowers To Your Loved One. 65

#138 Share the Remote Control 66

#139 Leave the Last Item 66

MAXIMIZE TIME SPENT TOGETHER 67

#140 Go for a Nature Walk Together 67

#141 Take an Evening Stroll. 67

#142 Take Lessons Together 67

#143 Watch the Sunset over the Ocean
or a Lake 68

#144 Buy a Bicycle Built for Two 68

#145 Go for a Canoe or Rowboat Ride. 68

#146 Go on a Nighttime Picnic 69

#147 Select a Pet Together 69

#148 Make Hot Chocolate on a Cold Day 69

#149 Take a Hay Ride 70

#150 Carve a Jack O' Lantern Together. 70

#151 Suggest a Formal Date Night. 70

#152 Attend an Arts and Crafts Festival 71

#153 Watch Home Movies Together 71

#154 Play "What If" 71

#155 Print a Photo Jigsaw Puzzle. 72

#156 Dress Alike on Halloween. 72

#157 Plan a Get-Away 72

#158 Watch a Romantic Movie Together 73

#159 Dedicate a Song on the Radio........... 73

#160 Express Your Love on a Button......... 73

#161 Plan a Picnic........................... 74

#162 Go Horseback Riding.................. 74

#163 Make S'mores Together................ 74

#164 Have a Barbeque....................... 74

#165 Put a Jigsaw Puzzle Together.......... 75

#166 Take a Hot Air Balloon Ride Together ... 75

#167 Plan a Game Night.................... 75

#168 Have Fun Together.................... 76

#169 Take on a Volunteer Project............ 77

CAPITALIZE ON SPONTANEITY 79

#170 Openly Flirt with Your Loved One...... 79

#171 Do the Unexpected.................... 79

#172 Act Like Newlyweds................... 79

#173 Do Something Special.................. 80

#174 Plan an Impromptu Meal Together...... 80

#175 Go for a Horse Drawn Carriage Ride..... 81

#176 Buy or Bake an I Love You Cookie...... 81

#177 Say I Love You with Flowers........... 81

#178 Dedicate a Song....................... 81

#179 Hold Hands When Walking............ 82

#180 Stop and Pick Wildflowers............. 82

#181 Buy a Spontaneous Present............ 82

#182 Give a Special Occasion Gift Certificate .. 83

#183 Buy a Balloon Heart 83

#184 Dance Spontaneously 84

#185 Display Your Love on a Cold Day 84

MAKE THE WORLD YOUR VEHICLE FOR LOVE 85

#186 Rent a Convertible Sports Car for
Your Next Trip 85

#187 Watch the New Year's Eve Ball Drop 85

#188 Create a Travel Map 85

#189 Go for a Day Trip 86

#190 Plan a Surprise Getaway 86

#191 Take a Trip to Las Vegas 87

#192 Visit a World Class City 87

#193 Kidnap Your Loved One 87

#194 Visit New Orleans 88

#195 Start a Trip Jar 88

#196 Plan a Trip to Venice, Italy 89

#197 Take a Cruise 89

#198 Eliminate a Bucket List Item 90

#199 Plan a Trip to a Romantic City 90

#200 Subscribe to Travel Magazines 90

GIVE THE GIFTS OF LOVE 91

#201 Gift a Car Detailing Certificate 91

#202 Declare "World's Greatest Lover" 91

#203 Buy Etched Glasses 91

#204 Make a Money Tree 92

#205 Give an Anniversary Ring 92

#206 Give a Heart-Shaped Paperweight 92

#207 Give a Gift Certificate of Love 93

#208 Have a Custom Quilt Made 93

#209 Send a Gift to Your Loved One 94

#210 Explore Your Genealogy 94

#211 Fill the Car with Balloons 94

#212 Purchase a Heart Umbrella 95

#213 Bring a Present When You Travel 95

#214 Buy Puzzle Books 95

#215 Give the Gift of Sensuality 95

#216 Give a Prepaid Gift or Charge Card 96

#217 Order a Customized Apron 96

#218 Buy a Favorite Fragrance 96

#219 Give a Money Box as a Present 96

#220 Purchase a Collectable 97

#221 Bake Cookies or Special Treats 97

#222 Get a Special Photo Framed 97

#223 Create a "Best Of" Listing 98

#224 Have Caricatures Drawn 98

#225 Give a Hobby Gift Certificate 98

#226 Get an Autograph 99

#227 Order a Coin for Special Occasions 99

#228 Create Customized Love Coupons 99

#229 Subscribe to a Favorite Publication 100

#230 Give a One-Year Club Membership 100

#231 Give a Copy of This Book 100

MY PLAN FOR LOVE WORKSHEET. 101

55 THINGS TO KNOW ABOUT YOUR LOVED ONE. 103

RESOURCES FOR LOVERS 107
Books. 107
Instructional Videos/Toys/Games/Clothing. . . . 110
Romantic/Sensuous/Sexy/Erotic Movies 110
Travel Magazines 111
Cruise Lines/Travel Agents 112

ABOUT THE AUTHOR 115

BOOKS BY ROBERT W. LUCAS 117

ABOUT ROBERT W. LUCAS ENTERPRISES . . . 119

REQUEST FOR REVIEWS 121

ORDER FORM: 231 Ways To Say I Love You . . . 123

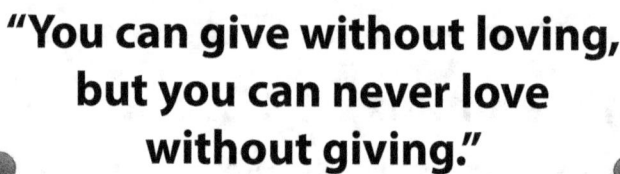

"You can give without loving, but you can never love without giving."

Unknown

PREFACE

MOST PEOPLE STRUGGLE to find their "true love" and then build and maintain a happy relationship. In my experience, this is because of three factors. The first is that people often define what love is differently. In many cases, especially at younger ages, love is often confused with infatuation or lust. Neither of these latter two feelings forms the basis for a lasting relationship.

Secondly, quite a few people have not learned to effectively listen and communicate verbally, non-verbally and in writing. As such, they do not know how to appropriately and regularly share their thoughts, needs and feelings to their spouse or significant other.

The third issue is that many people get too caught up in other aspects of their life (e.g., child rearing, career, hobbies, surfing the Internet and other personal interests). Unfortunately, this can lead to unconsciously relegating a spouse or significant other to a secondary position in their lives and as a result receive minimal attention in the relationship. It is no wonder that the divorce rates have skyrocketed over the years.

Like many of you reading this book, I have experienced peaks and valleys related to love. My first love was at age 16. She was a fair-haired, beautiful creature who swept me off my feet. I used the phrase "love at first sight," to describe our relationship and with the wild-eyed abandonment of youth, we flew head on into what we believed was "the love of our lives." As I recall, we spent a lot of time cuddling, kissing, talking about whatever and being on the phone swearing our undying love for hours. We planned to marry after high school graduation and to have six children. Unfortunately, at that age, we did not spend time talking about realistic life issues or getting to the essence of what a relationship is built on. Alas, it was not to be and at age 17 she informed me that we were parting and that she was going off with another. While I was crushed, in retrospect, it was the best thing that could have happened. Like most people of that age, I was not prepared for a life-long relationship. Instead, I went on to travel the world and do things I never even dreamed of as a teenager. Much later in life, I married and divorced, went through a series of other relationships where I honed my relationship knowledge and skills and ultimately, met my soul mate (M.J.—a.k.a. known affectionately as "**My Joy**"). We married two years later, and while we have encountered the challenges that many couples do, we continually work to keep our relationship fresh and strive to regularly build new memories.

My purpose in writing this book is to share ideas and strategies that anyone can apply to help develop and nurture a meaningful relationship. By applying these techniques you can help create an atmosphere of effective communication, trust and love with your spouse or significant other.

I have found that the key in keeping an affinity for one another strong is to recognize that a relationship and friendship with your partner develops over time and is not something to take lightly or for granted. It takes continual effort by both parties to support and convey love, needs, wants and expectations. If you want to succeed with your loved one, you cannot demonstrate the attitude portrayed by the husband in the following joke that I heard years ago.

> *An old man and his wife of 50 years went to a marriage counselor because they were having difficulties in their relationship.*

The woman cried loudly as she poured her heart out to the counselor. "He never tells me he loves me anymore," she quipped.

Confused, the befuddled husband looked at her with amazement and replied, "Didn't I tell you I loved you when we got married?"

She replied "Well . . . yes."

To which he said, "Well, if it changes, I'll let you know."

The message here is that just because you know that you love your partner does not mean that he or she knows how you feel. Each person is different, unique and has distinct personality traits and levels of emotional need. If you do not know how your partner approaches relationships, you can simply ask, listen to their response and discuss ways the two of you can better communicate personal needs and strengthen your relationship. Do not assume all is well. Take the time to check in periodically to discuss ways that you can both strengthen and renew the relationship.

A final thought about love and relationships that I hope you will heed as much as my wife and I do. Life is too short not to have fun and enjoy each other. Get out together, enjoy things together and find ways to build new cherished memories. Make sure that each time you part or end a conversation, that you tell your partner how you feel and that you love him or her. It may be the last opportunity you ever get. Live, Laugh and Love Long!

Best Wishes,
Bob Lucas

**Relationships=
Two People;
One Heart**

INTRODUCTION

"Try to be a rainbow in someone's cloud."
Maya Angelou

THE PURPOSE OF *231 Ways to Say I Love You* is to provide a convenient reference source and reminder to anyone who is in love with another person and is looking for ways to add to or rekindle the excitement in their relationship. In it you will find many easy-to-apply, practical and romantic strategies for letting your spouse or significant other know that you love, desire and appreciate him or her.

The format of the book is simple and straightforward with a listing of the 231 suggested love strategies arranged into seven relationship-related categories. Unlike many books on this topic, *231 Ways to Say I Love You* builds on the author's personal experience in relationships, as well as, expertise, research and knowledge that he has gained related to building effective interpersonal relationships. He has written thirty-three other books that delve into strategies for communicating more effectively and building better relationships in many environments. Additionally, he has been a consultant, trainer and speaker to thousands of people from various diverse backgrounds for over four decades. In those roles, he has shared ideas and strategies for better understanding the behavior that people exhibit in a variety of settings so that clients might more effectively understand and interact with others.

As you read these pages, think of other techniques that you have effectively used or seen others use in the past that let loved ones know that they were valued and cherished. Throughout the book you will discover ways to communicate your feelings to others in fun, practical and simple ways. At the end of the book, you will find a "My Plan for Love" worksheet for capturing your own ideas for giving "love messages" on any given day. There are also dozens of useful resources listed at the end of the book to supplement the ideas and information you will read in *231 Ways to Say I Love You*.

In addition to creative ideas for enhancing your love life and strengthening your relationship, you will find quotes related to love and relationships. These can be thought provoking for you and might also be copied to provide periodic messages of love to your spouse or significant other. Use the quotes on napkins, notes, in greeting cards or in other creative locations to let your loved one know how special and important he or she is to you.

"I love you without knowing how, or when, or from where. I love you simply, without problems or pride: I love you in this way because I do not know any other way of loving but this, in which there is no I or you, so intimate that your hand upon my chest is my hand, so intimate that when I fall asleep your eyes close."

Pablo Neruda, 100 Love Sonnets

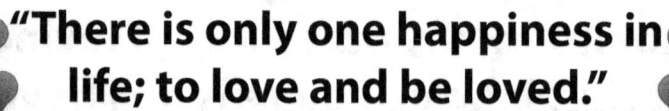

"There is only one happiness in life; to love and be loved."

George Sand

INTENSIFY YOUR RELATIONSHIP

 **#1   Work to Build Trust**

All relationships are built on trust and require a commitment on the part of both partners. Building it with another person takes a lot of time and effort. Unfortunately, after all your efforts and good intentions to build trust, it can be destroyed or negatively impacted in a second or with one misstep on your part. If you fail to recognize this fact, you might inhibit or destroy your partner's trust in you by seemingly simple or unconscious acts or failures.

> *"Remember the Three R's of Relationships:*
> *Respect for self;*
> *Respect for others;*
> *Responsibility for all your actions."*
> Unknown

Some strategies for effectively building trust include the following.

Listen openly. When a loved one has something to share, take the time to listen openly and objectively. If you are working on a time-sensitive project or task, ask if what he or she has to say can be postponed. If that is agreeable, set a specific time and then keep that appointment to hear what is on your loved one's mind. A word of caution, if you ask for a postponement, watch non-verbal cues closely to make sure that your spouse or significant other is not saying it is okay verbally, but signaling with body cues that the conversation cannot wait.

Keep your word. If you promise to do something or go somewhere with your loved one, fulfill your commitment(s).

Be truthful. One of the quickest ways to destroy trust is to lie or keep secrets from your spouse or significant other. This does not mean that you have to share every thought or experience that you have. Rather, you should work to build a strong communication channel where you come to an agreement on what types of things are acceptable or not in the relationship.

Be open to change. Change does not come naturally for most people and is hard for many to accept. One of the biggest complaints that some people in relationships often voice is that they feel like things have become commonplace or stagnant and that the fun or spark has disappeared. Work together to keep the magic alive in your relationship by being willing to try new things and "mix it up" regularly.

"The Best Proof of Love Is Trust."
Dr. Joyce Brothers

Empathize. In a 24/7/365 world where there never seems to be time to do everything that you need or want to do, it is likely that there will be times in which it feels like the world is closing in on you or your partner. Be aware of pressures that your loved one may be experiencing or is voicing. Listen and emphasize with him or her. This sometimes means that you have to "back off" and give your loved one time to relax in his or her own way, resolve issues in their own preferred manner or just be alone to process information or ideas or issues.

Intensify Your Relationship

Support Your Loved One. Mutual support is an important element in any relationship. Do not fall prey to talking negatively about your loved one to friends or others. Also, if someone verbally attacks your spouse or significant other, even if he or she is not present, you should defend him or her. Failure to do so could cause relationship damage if your loved one later finds out about your lack of support.

 **#2 Show Respect**

Respect has to be earned by you and your loved one and is an important element in any successful relationship. Aside from taking personal responsibility for what you each do and say, there are subtle ways to show that you respect one another.

> *"Trust is involved in all basic elements of a healthy relationship: namely, love (respect and consideration for another person), communication, commitment and honesty."*
> Harold Duarte-Bernhardt

The following are some simple strategies for demonstrating respect:

Thank your spouse or significant other. When your loved one says kind things to you, demonstrates caring and loving behavior, or performs a task for you or other family members, acknowledge their efforts. This includes when performance of routine tasks (e.g., house cleaning or running errands for you) or exhibiting unexpected behavior like a spontaneous kiss or hug or telling you that you are loved.

Avoid always trying to get your way. Partnerships are about win-win. Both parties need to feel that there is an opportunity for input and to "have it their way" on a regular basis. Be willing to negotiate and in some instances compromise in your daily life and when disagreements surface. When possible, be willing to say "yes" when your loved one says or suggests something, even if you do not totally agree. There is an old adage . . ."A happy wife is a happy life." This applies with husbands and significant others as well.

> **"Intense love does not measure, it just gives."**
> Mother Teresa

Avoid derogatory "terms of endearment" to describe your spouse or significant other. Some couples use terms like "my old lady/old man" or other similar negative labels to refer to their partner and believe (or say) these are terms of endearment.

Unfortunately, at some point, your partner may start to feel that this is a put down or term of disrespect. Also, when others hear such language they might make the assumption that one person is being disrespectful and uncaring by using such language. With all the other kinder and traditional names that couples use (e.g., my better half, my love, my sweetheart, my spouse, my bride, or girlfriend/boyfriend) you may want to look for a more affectionate way to describe the person you love in order to indicate that you respect him or her.

Avoid put-downs. Do not get in the habit of picking on your loved one's shortcomings or misfortunes and degrading or talking down to her or him, especially, in the presence of others. This will likely ultimately affect their self-esteem and could impact the level of trust that is present in your relationship. If your spouse or significant other is less educated, has failed at some business venture, been laid off from work, or has other background characteristics that might be played upon to embarrass or shame for some reason, avoid bringing these up. Accept your partner for who he or she is, not what you expect or want him or her to be. That should be the person with whom you initially fell in love. If it is not, there may actually be some flaw in your own character and judgement and you may want to consider counseling and/or leaving the relationship for the sake of you and your partner.

> **"When you say, 'I love you,' mean it."**
> Unknown

Praise in public. Most people appreciate it when someone, especially their significant other, recognizes and praises their achievements and ideas in front of other people. When such opportunities occur, make sure that you recognize and appreciate what your loved one has done or accomplished.

Never resort to negative labeling or name-calling. Everyone gets frustrated or irritated with their partner from time to time. In many instances, this is caused because or outside influences or events that carry over into the relationship (e.g., money, family members, workplace issues and other stressors). There is no reason to take out resentment on the ones you love or use derogatory terms (e.g., stupid, ignorant, lazy, or profane terms). This is especially important when there are others present who might witness the exchange (e.g., children, friends, relatives or bystanders).

Do your share of household chores. Even if one person is a stay at home mom or dad, pitch in to shoulder some of the workload around the house, especially, if you have children. You may even divvy up some responsibilities. For example, you might adopt a practice of the person who cooks, does not also have to do the dishes. You can always switch off the cooking function every other night.

> *"When you realize you've made a mistake,*
> *Take immediate steps to correct it."*
> Unknown

Ask for and value your loved one's opinion. Nobody is perfect or has all the right answers to any problem or situation. When a project, issue, concern or other opportunity arises where a second opinion would be useful, be sure to include your spouse or significant other in the mix of opinions that you solicit. You will often be pleasantly surprised by their honest, open, constructive feedback and he or she will likely be appreciative that you took the time to ask and consider their advice.

Regularly demonstrate your love. Use strategies such as the ones outlined in this book to regularly show your loved one that he or she is the most important person in your life. Show him or her how much they are cherished and that you are happy to have been chosen as their life partner.

 **#3   Accept Responsibility**

There are many times in life when something happens or goes wrong and it is not your fault. In those instances when you do or say something that is wrong or creates challenges in your relationship, you should take responsibility and say "I'm sorry." This small effort goes a long way toward building the trust that you read about earlier and to helping mend hurt feelings and prevent possible resentment.

> *"Love isn't something you find. Love is something that finds you."*
> Loretta Young

 **#4 Respect Privacy**

Relationships can sometimes seem confining, especially when first starting out and both you and your loved one are trying to determine the boundaries and get to know one another. Take some time to discuss what is acceptable in your relationship. Most people like their own "space" and when they do not get it, might start to resent intrusions and ultimately withdraw from a relationship. This is probably why we often hear of people establishing "man caves" or "she sheds" as some they strive to stake out their own territory in a relationship.

Do you remember how you resented your parents, caregivers or siblings entering your bedroom or private space and going through your personal belongings as a teenager? Well, you likely have not gotten past those feelings totally. As a show of respect, ask permission before you go through your loved one's personal belongings, car, wallet or purse, listen to their voicemail or read their email/text messages, or enter the bathroom when they are using it.

> *"I love you, and because I love you, I would sooner have you hate me for telling you the truth than adore me for telling you lies."*
> Pietro Aretino

 **#5 Be a Positive Role Model**

If you have children in the home, remember that they are always watching your interactions with your loved one. Whether you realize it or not, they are picking up on your actions, language, and behavior toward your spouse or significant other. Make sure that the lessons they learn regarding relationships revolve around the concepts of respect, positive verbal and nonverbal communication, active listening, and behavior that send a message of love and trust for others.

 #6 Create a Couple's "To Do" List

Instead of New Year's resolutions, sit with your loved one on New Year's Day and create a list of 52 things (one for each week of the year) that you are both going to do as a couple to strengthen your relationship during the year. You can choose some ideas from this book, research others, or come up with your own strategies.

 **#7 Read Relationship "How To" Books**

Everyone can learn with an open mind. Look for books that discuss strategies for stronger relationships (e.g., like this one) and share with your loved one. After you both have read a book, discuss its content and ways to apply what was learned.

"A healthy relationship is built on unwavering trust."
Beau Mirchoff

 **Overlook Your Pet Peeves**

While everyone likely has something that is irritating to a loved one, it is not usually grounds for a major argument or continued nagging. If your spouse or significant other has an annoying habit or trait; calmly share that it bothers you. Ask him or her to try to cease or curtail the behavior. If an occasional slip and fall back into the habit occurs, try to overlook it rather than saying or doing something that might hurt feelings or cause other issues in the relationship. If the behavior is a serious issue and you really have challenges accepting it, and the two of you cannot work it out, see a counselor yourself or get your loved one to go with you to one in order to try to resolve the issue.

 **Praise Your Loved One**

People in relationships often get too comfortable with one another and unconsciously take their partner for granted. On a daily basis, make an effort to recognize the things that your spouse or significant other does and their accomplishments. "Brag" about your sweetheart in front of friends and family. It might be something like talking about the beautiful flower bed that they planted over the weekend or some milestone achieved. If your spouse or significant other is not unusually embarrassed in such situations, once you introduce the topic, put the spotlight on him or her to share more details about the accomplishment.

 **#10   Don't Always Be Right**

Even if you suspect that your loved one is not totally accurate when telling a story to others, do not be quick to correct what was said if it is really an insignificant point.

> *"Don't smother each other.*
> *No one can grow in the shade."*
> Leo Buscagli

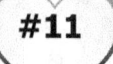 **#11   Let Your Loved One Choose a Movie**

Take your spouse or significant other to a theatre and let him or her select the movie you will watch. If you would rather stay home to watch a movie, let your loved one decide on the title. Don't forget the drinks and snacks!

 **#12   Let Your Emotional Guard Down**

Share your feelings on a regular basis. If you cannot let your loved one in on your inner thoughts and feelings, you are likely going to have problems with the relationship. Trust that what you say will be taken in through an empathetic ear and that your partner loves, cares, and supports you. This is the basis of a sound relationship.

 **#13   Attend Family Functions**

When you become part of someone's life you naturally take on certain social responsibilities, such as, attending family functions (e.g., weddings, funerals, celebrations, holiday meals, and picnics). This might be uncomfortable or difficult depending on your personality style and own family background. Even so, it is important to your relationship that you make a sincere effort to participate in your loved one's family events without complaining. Look at these events as opportunities to learn more about your spouse or significant other and to strengthen your relationship. By taking part in such activities and going as a partner, you subliminally say *I Love You* and indicate that your loved one and his or her feelings are important to you.

> *"If you find someone to love in life,
> then hang onto that love."*
> Princess Diana

 **#14 Take Your In-Laws to Lunch**

Show interest in your loved one's family by offering to take various in-laws to lunch occasionally. In addition to bonding with these people, you will also potentially learn more about your spouse or significant other when you do this.

 **#15 Give a "Thank You" Card**

Buy a box of thank you cards and keep these on hand. When your loved one does something special (e.g., cooks a special meal, cleans up your mess, or goes out of the way to do something for you) give a *Thank You* card with a personal note inside expressing how much you appreciate and love him or her.

 **#16 Don't Unload Your Frustrations**

Instead of greeting your loved one after work with negative events that occurred during your day, smile, give a big hug, kiss and say how happy you are to see him or her. Chances are, they experienced some negativity too during the day and just need relax and know that you are there to share your love.

"Trust is the first step to love."
Munshi Premchand

 **#17 Acknowledge Your Mistakes**

We all make mistakes. When you do or say something that causes a riff in your relationship, take immediate steps to fix the problem before it grows and leads to other issues. The words "I was wrong" and "I am sorry" can go a long way to diffusing a potential volatile situation.

 **#18 Remove the Television**

Get the television out of the bedroom. Use the bedroom for communication, sensuality and sleeping. Sleep science research shows that the optimal conditions for a good night's sleep is a completely darkened room (this includes removing clock and night lights), with 68 degrees Fahrenheit temperature and total silence.

 **#19 Start a Tradition**

It does not matter if you have been together one month or for twenty years, work with your loved one to decide on a tradition that will be used for special events. For example, you might get away for a weekend every anniversary or decorate a Christmas tree with special or customized ornaments that you collect when you take trips. For example, my wife and I have been collecting giraffe ornaments for years and only have those on our Christmas tree each year. This tradition makes it fun to decorate for the holidays, is a good conversation point with guests and gives us something to look for when we travel as we search for new, unique additions.

> *"Infatuation is when you find someone who is absolutely perfect. Love is when you realize that they aren't and it doesn't matter."*
>
> Unknown

 **#20 Kiss and Make Up**

Most couples have disagreements or arguments. When this occurs with your loved one, make sure that you take time to apologize and discuss what caused the point of contention afterwards. This helps keep the communication lines open and potentially prevents unresolved issues from festering and coming up again in the future. If you were at fault, you might even get a greeting card that says *I'm sorry* and write a personal note in it expressing your love.

 **#21 Remember That You Are Partners**

Never forget that you are a partner with your loved one. You must both do your part to build and keep the relationship strong.

Merriam-Webster's dictionary defines *partner* as:

"One associated with another especially in an action; either of two persons who dance together; one of two or more persons who play together in a game against an opposing side; a person with whom one shares an intimate relationship; *one member of a couple.*"

> *"Love is the only gold."*
> Alfred Lord Tennyson

 **#22 Commit to Improvement**

Pick a date within thirty days as a starting point and put it on your calendar. Agree that you will both make a concerted effort to improve your relationship starting that day by signing up for a class, reading and discussing a book (e.g., relationship skills, sexuality, or communication), going to a counselor, or taking other proactive steps to learn more about interpersonal communication, relationships and how to make your partnership stronger. Repeat this process once a year.

BRING BACK THE ROMANCE

 **#23 Become a Committed Romantic**

Many people in relationships become romantic for limited times on occasions like anniversaries, birthdays, Valentine's Day and other special occasions. While this is nice and commendable to a point, romance is not something you should put away after an occasion and take out for the next. Work to become truly romantic around your loved one all the time. Make a conscious effort to do things on a regular basis that say *I love you* and shows your partner that he or she is not only special, but also the center of your life.

"The person you're meant to be with will never have to be chased, begged or given an ultimatum."
Mandy Hale

 **#24 Make a List of Things You Like**

Liking and loving go hand in hand. Make a list of seven things that you like about your loved one. Start the list with "I Like You Because . . ." Write *I Love You* at the end and attach the list to the bathroom mirror some morning before your partner wakes up.

 **#25 Use Heart Shaped Ice Cubes**

For Valentine's Day or whenever you want to send a love message, make heart shaped ice cubes and put these in your loved one's drink. These might become a nonverbal invitation used when you would like to have an intimate evening with your spouse or significant other. You can find ice trays in the shape of hearts at many department stores and on the Internet.

"Love will keep us together"
Howard Greenfield and Neil Sedaka

 **#26 Leave a Personal Recorded Message**

When you know your loved one has turned off his or her cell phone or will not answer, call and leave a personal message letting him or her know how much he or she is loved and appreciated. You might even leave an invitation for an intimate dinner and evening together.

 **#27 Print and Frame a Noted Poem**

Purchase some nice stationary. Use it to print and frame a copy Elizabeth Barrett Browning's poem "How Do I Love Thee," or another of your favorites, and give it as a gift to your loved one for no special reason.

 **#28 Write a Love Poem or Song**

If you look at the words on greeting cards or in love poems and songs, you quickly realize that they are likely the result of some personal event experienced by the writer of those pieces. Each person feels love in individual ways. Take the time to write down your innermost thoughts about the relationship you share with your loved one so that it is clear to him or her how you really feel. Give this personal written gift for no reason at all or on a special occasion.

You might write about the emotions you felt the first time you saw or met your spouse or significant other, the first time you were intimate, when you proposed, the day you were married, or some other significant life event that you experienced together. As you write, address the qualities that you cherish and the feelings you have for your loved one, how he or she makes you feel, or other thoughts. The important point is that you are speaking from your heart to your loved one's heart.

> *"Love is when the other person's happiness is more important than your own."*
> H. Jackson Brown Jr.

 **#29 Sprinkle Rose Petals Over the Bed**

As a prelude to an intimate night on a special occasion (outlined in this book) buy a dozen roses and sprinkle the petals leading into the bedroom and over the bed.

 **#30   Send a Telegram**

Telegrams are "old school" technology and many people have never received one in today's world. That is what makes these messages so special. Send a telegram formally inviting your loved one on a date. If it is a special occasion, consider picking him or her up in a limousine.

 **#31   Download Music of Love**

Take the time to research 15–20 songs that focus on the message of love and record these. Wrap the recording in a small gift box with colorful paper and give it to your loved one along with a greeting card that espouses your love. You can do this on a special occasion (e.g., birthday or anniversary) or just as a surprise gift for no special reason at all. If you have access to radio stations that have romantic music shows (e.g., Delilah); they are a great source for identifying possible songs.

"Do all things with love."
Og Mandino

 **#32   Put Your Initials in Concrete**

If you have a new concrete driveway, patio deck or sidewalk poured, draw a heart and put your initials and those of your loved one along with the date before the cement dries. Another option is to pour a concrete square in a flower bed, join with your spouse or significant other in putting your palm prints, initials and the date in it. The nice part about this approach is that if you ever move, you can take the memento with you.

 ### #33 Post Your Message of Love

Before going to work or after returning home, take a pad of 'Sticky Notes" and spell out "I Luv U!" on the bathroom mirror or other place where your loved one will readily spot it.

A variation of this is to spell out other messages to greet your spouse or significant other when he or she returns from a trip or has been gone for a period of time. Possible messages include:

>*I Love You*
>
>*I Missed You*
>
>*You Are Loved*
>
>*Welcome Home*

 ### #34 Create a Special Award

Go to a local trophy shop that creates custom awards, select a trophy or medal that you like and have it inscribed for your loved one. You might use something like "World's Greatest *spouse, friend, father/mother, lover*" or other designation that you prefer.

> **"Most folks are as happy as they make up their minds to be."**
> Abraham Lincoln

 **#35   Write Your Own Wedding Vows**

Make your special day even more meaningful by writing your wedding vows from your heart. If you are already married, use these to get renew your vows and get remarried.

 **#36   Give Your Loved One a Sign**

When your loved one returns after a trip, put a colorful poster board sign decorated with colorful flowers, hearts or other images by the driveway or door to the house that they will use. You can add whatever message you'd like. For example, "Welcome Home!" or "I/We Missed You."

 **#37   Get a Tattoo**

Get a tattoo with a heart with an arrow through it and your initials and those of your loved one in it. In recent years, such images have become more socially accepted on both sexes. If you would rather not be permanently inked, get a temporary version (available on the Internet). Have a photo made of you and your spouse or significant other with your new addition so that you have a lasting record of it once it wears off.

> *"Your words are my food, your breath my wine.*
> *You are everything to me."*
> Sarah Bernhardt

 **Write I Love You in the Sand**

The next time that you go to a beach, let the world see your love by writing "I LOVE *(insert loved one's name)*" in the sand. Maybe even build a sandcastle together next to the message.

 **Share Your Love with the World**

With the advent of social media, many people have taken to the Internet to share their feelings and love for their spouse or significant other with the world. Through YouTube, Facebook and numerous other outlets, they post photos, poems and messages that profess their love to another. There have even been some recent studies which indicate that couples who do this for over six months are more likely to stay together because they have coupled in front of others and feel more of a commitment.

 **Recreate Your First Date**

On the anniversary of your first date, recreate that event and the activities of that day to remind your loved one how important it was to you.

 **Write Love Messages in the Snow**

If you are in a snowy region, take advantage and write love messages in the winter snow. Build a huge mound of snow and pack the front part of it tightly and smoothly. Get some food coloring or tempera paint (from a craft or school supply store). Put your message on the snow face so that is the first thing your loved one sees when he or she returns home from work or a trip.

"Grow old along with me. The best is yet to be."
Robert Browning

 **#42   Buy a Boutonnière and Corsage**

When going out on a special date with your loved one in which you both dress more formally, buy one another a boutonnière and corsage to add to the spark of the event. Pretend you are going to the prom with your loved one and maybe go dancing after dinner.

 **#43   Play Hooky on Valentine's Day or Anniversary**

Take the entire day off from work on Valentine's Day or the anniversary of your first date or wedding. Spend the day with your partner doing whatever you choose to make it a special occasion for both of you.

 **#44   Get Regular Formal Portraits Made**

Capture special times together by having formal portraits made of you and your loved one. This is easy on a cruise ship since they have photographers all over the ship and on formal nights to capture photos. If you own a digital camera with an automatic timer and tripod, you can create your own images and have these printed at local photo shops, labs or on a computer.

Bring Back The Romance

"Love is the condition in which the happiness of another person is essential to your own."
Robert Heinlein

 **#45 Order Customized License Plates**

If your state sells customized automobile license plates, order one for your car(s) with both your initials separated by a "+" symbol. If you both have cars, reverse the order of the initials for each car, as appropriate.

 **#46 Rent a Beach Bungalow**

Take a getaway where you rent a beach bungalow or hotel room on the beach. Have a great intimate evening, go to sleep spooning (curled together against one another) and wake up to the sound of the rolling tide before going for a breakfast or ordering room service for just the two of you.

 **#47 Have a Bumper Sticker Made**

Many tourist areas, flea markets and artisan venues have vendors who create customized bumper stickers on the spot. Think of a special message that you would like to put on a rear window or bumper for the world to see (*e.g., I Love My Spouse!*).

 **#48 Renew Your Wedding Vows**

You do not have to wait until you are older to renew your wedding vows. Select an anniversary (e.g., 1st, 5th,

10th, 15th or 20th), send out invitations to friends and relatives and have a small celebration of your life together thus far. Write new vows or stick to more traditional religious ones.

Unfortunately, many people decide to wait for some long-term date (e.g., 50th anniversary) to recommit to one another. Sadly, something could happen to your partner if you wait long periods and you will likely regret never moving forward on your plans to renew your vows.

If you'd rather keep the event personal and unique, take a cruise and arrange for the ship's captain to officiate the vows.

"Love is like the wind, you can't see it but you can feel it."
Nicholas Sparks

#49 Send a Series of Greeting Cards

Buy seven romantic greeting cards and mail one each day of the week leading up to an anniversary. Make sure to use the U.S. Postal service "Two Hearts; One Love" Forever stamps if you are mailing in the United States.

#50 Cuddle While Watching Television

Put your arm around your loved ones shoulder, hold hands, or have him or her lay their head on your lap as you stroke their head or scratch their back gently while watching television.

 **#51 Place the Winning Bid at an Auction**

If your spouse or significant other indicates a preference for something being offered at a silent or live auction, make sure that you are the high bidder to get that item for him or her.

> *"If you want a love message to be heard, it has to be sent out. To keep a lamp burning, we have to keep putting oil in it."*
> Mother Teresa

 **#52 Keep a Relationship Scrapbook**

Clip articles from newspapers or other publications (e.g., organizational newsletters or blogs) about significant events in your life and that of your loved one. These might include wedding, birth of a child, promotion announcements, appointments to boards or other volunteer initiatives, articles about activities in which one (or both) of you were involved, tickets from special events that you attended, or anything else that you think is special about you and your loved one.

 **#53 Purchase Customized Coffee Mugs**

Get matching coffee mugs or glasses with whatever message you prefer. Potential messages might be *His, Hers, The King, The Queen, Mine, Yours,* or whatever cute and clever message you prefer. These might also be creative sayings or to commemorate professions (e.g., nursing, military branch, etc).

 **#54 Say "Goodnight" and "I Love You"**

Make the last conscious thought of your day be about your spouse or significant other. If you are not physically together call, email or connect through the Internet to tell her or him "goodnight" and "I Love You." If you are together, take time to kiss and say these words before drifting off to sleep. In a crazy hectic world, you never know what can happen and you may never get a second chance to take these actions.

 **#55 Buy Flannel Sheets**

Get a nice set of cozy sheets for your bed. Snuggle in the cold parts of the year or just crank up the air conditioning if you live in the tropics.

TAP THE ELEMENT OF SURPRISE

 **#56 Splurge for Front Row Seats**

Surprise your loved one by spending some extra money to get prime seats for a music concert or performance that he or she really wants to see. Make the event even more special by going to Broadway in New York, Las Vegas, or on one of the larger cruise ships that offer full Broadway shows, to see the show.

*"When you truly love someone,
you don't judge them by their past.
You leave it there. Just be happy
that their future is with you."*

Unknown

 **#57 Give a Calendar as a Present**

Buy a calendar with photos of something your loved one likes (e.g., a specific animal, cars, areas of the world, or sports team). Mark important dates for the entire year on it. For example, family birthdays, the date you first met, anniversaries, planned trips or whatever else you want to ensure that is not forgotten. Give this as a gift at Christmas or some other appropriate time near the end or beginning of the year. If you want to really make the calendar special, take photos of the two of you in special places you have visited and have these made into a custom calendar at a local photography lab or store.

 **Do Something Nice**

Relationships grow one day at a time. Make a conscious effort to do at least one nice thing for your loved one each day.

 **Treat to a Round of Golf**

If your loved one plays golf, either take him or her for a round or (if you do not play) give a gift certificate for a round of golf at a local course.

 **Send a Singing Mylar Balloon**

Like greeting cards, some Mylar balloons now have imbedded songs inside. You can order these online and at some novelty and party stores that sell helium balloons. As these products become more popular you will likely have little trouble locating a source.

> *"Love doesn't make the world go 'round.*
> *Love is what makes the ride worthwhile."*
> Franklin P. Jones

 **Surprise with a Special Treat**

Surprise your spouse or significant other on a weekend and take Him or her to get their favorite ice cream, iced coffee, pizza or whatever else you know they enjoy. Take along a copy of *4,000 Questions for Getting to Know Anyone and Everyone* by Barbra Ann Kipler **and take turns selecting questions to discuss in order to learn more about one another.**

 **#62 Declare a Special Day**

Proclaim a specific day as one that celebrates your spouse or significant other and then treat him or her as royalty. You might cook breakfast, lunch, and dinner, clean all the dishes after meals, take your loved one out for a movie or other event, or prepare a romantic intimate night (as discussed elsewhere in this book). To make the day more special, create a poster or banner with the day's title (e.g., King/Queen of the Day, Best Father/Mother/Spouse Day or other title you prefer). You could tie this idea with the "Create a Special Award" strategy found in this book.

 **#63 Pack a Special Surprise**

If your spouse or significant other typically packs a lunch or snack for work, secretly slip in a special note with a personal message (e.g., Have a great day!, I Love You!, or I'll be waiting for you to get home!) into their food container. An alternative is to slip in a love poem you wrote or found online or a greeting card that expresses how you feel about your sweetheart.

*"Love is not only something you feel.
It is something you do."*
David Wilkerson

 **#64   Surprise the Traveler**

If your spouse or significant other is leaving on a trip without you, put a surprise greeting card inside his or her suitcase, on their car dash, or simply hand it to him or her as they walk out the door.

To do this, buy a greeting card that has a message pertinent to your feelings about your loved one and write a personal emotional note inside and sign. Next, if your loved one is a book reader and will be taking public transportation and have time to read, get a copy of a book that they have mentioned that they want to read or that you believe they might enjoy. If their trip does not involve traveling through airport or other security checkpoints, you might even wrap the book and card in heart-decorated or other appropriate paper (the kind normally found in stores at Valentine's Day).

If your loved one is not a book reader, but will have access to a computer or other USB port source, record a number of love songs that send messages you would like to convey onto a thumb drive or other appropriate recording source and give it to your partner as he or she departs, along with the card mentioned above.

"Believe in love at first sight."
Unknown

 **#65   Get Up Early and Go for Pastries**

As a special treat, occasionally wake up earlier than your loved one and go out for coffee and pastries then wake him or her to enjoy your treat together.

Tap The Element Of Surprise

 **Hide Messages of Love in Easter Eggs**

On Easter, surprise your loved one with a basket containing favorite types of candy and some plastic eggs containing a variety of love messages or poems inside.

 **Put an Advertisement in the Newspaper**

Newspapers advertisements are not just for selling products, announcing weddings or listing obituaries. Contact your local newspaper advertising department and place an ad for any special event or just to declare your love publically. On the date that the advertisement is to first appear, get a copy of the paper, circle the ad and place it on the breakfast table for your loved one to find when he or she comes to eat. Add a bit more romance by having a single rose (or other favorite flower) in a vase next to the paper.

> *"Love conquers all things;*
> *let us surrender to love."*
>
> Virgil

 **Hire a High School Band or Choir**

High school bands and choirs often do fund raisers for trips to their competitions. Check with some local high schools to hire their band or choir to come to a special celebration (e.g., birthday or promotion) for your loved one as a surprise. Have the musicians or singers perform some favorite songs.

A variation is to find some local musicians who play for small events in your area. You can often find these people playing at mall events, fund raisers, in restaurants or in other local venues and on the Internet.

 **#69   Send Letters or Postcards**

No matter whether you are gone away from your loved one for a week or a month, make the effort to send a card or letter updating him or her and sharing your love and appreciation. Email, eCards and cell phone calls are easy communication tools, but it takes added effort to write something, get a stamp on it and mail it. This small gesture will likely not be lost on your loved one and is something that many people store and keep for decades. You can't accomplish the same emotional result as easily with a cell recording or email.

 **#70   Plan a Surprise Airport Greeting**

When your spouse or significant other is returning from a trip alone via an airplane, plan a surprise greeting at the luggage claim area. Take flowers or a small wrapped welcome home gift, then spirit him or her off to a nice restaurant for lunch or dinner before heading home for another surprise in the bedroom.

> *"We're never so vulnerable than when we trust someone —but paradoxically, if we cannot trust, neither canwe find love or joy."*
> Walter Anderson

 **#71 Rent a Billboard**

On a really special occasion where you are thrilled to be in a loving relationship with your spouse or significant other, why not share the news by renting a billboard. Proclaim your love, propose, announce some special event or just put your name and that of your loved one in huge letters with a heart image along with some personal message. Talk about visual impact!

Variations of this strategy are to put an advertisement on the side of a bus or taxi cab that tours your local area or take out an ad on the movie screens shown in your local area. When you know where the ad will be running, make sure your spouse or significant other sees it.

 **#72 Prepare a Surprise Greeting**

Surprise your loved one when they come home from work by printing a poster or banner that says "*(loved one's name)* Appreciation Day" and have it proudly displayed where it will be seen when your sweetheart walks through the door. Also, greet your spouse or significant other with a big smile, kiss and hug and share that you missed and love him or her very much. Have a special meal prepared along with a favorite entrée, wine/drink, and dessert.

> *"It's not what we have in life,*
> *but who we have in our life that matters."*
> J. M. Laurence

 **#73 Send a Congratulatory Card**

Following some successful effort (e.g., finishing a project, completing a task around the house, giving a speech or presentation, or getting a promotion) send a congratulatory card to your loved one. Include personal words of encouragement along with a message that you support, believe in and love him or her. If you prefer, you can send an eCard instead of a written one, but it might not convey the same degree of passion.

 **#74 Send a Singing Telegram**

Like their written cousins, singing telegrams are a novel, fun and easy way to send a message to your loved one. Depending on the area in which you live, you may be able to find services in your local area to deliver one of these.

> *"Trust in what you love, continue to do it,*
> *and it will take you where you need to go."*
> Natalie Goldberg

 **#75 Have a Special Valentine's Day**

Plan a surprise celebration for Valentine's Day by making a poster or banner that proclaims *I Love You* and hang it in the garage or house to greet your loved one upon arrival from work. Also, drape bushes and hedges in the yard with red holiday lights or hang heart shaped party lights around the house or patio. Add to the festivities by purchasing an oversized Valentine's card and adding a person message of love, buying appropriate party favors to hang or place on the dinner table, cooking a special meal, and planning an intimate evening or using one of the other strategies highlighted in this book to demonstrate your love.

 **#76 Create a Photo Screen Image**

Go through photos of you with your loved one together and select one you really like or that brings back pleasant memories. Surprise your spouse or significant other by saving the image as a background screen on your computer and that of your loved one.

 **#77 Create a Video of Love**

For a special occasion (e.g., Mother's/Father's Day, birthday, or anniversary) contact close friends and relatives to ask for photos that they have of your spouse or significant other throughout their lifetime together. Use these to create a photo montage of their life accompanied by a musical background of your loved one's favorite music. An alternative to this is to video family members and friends talking about what your loved one has meant to them and any favorite memories of their relationship. Play your masterpiece at a party or other event where friends and family have gathered and present it to your loved one afterwards. Just make sure that you do not include things that might embarrass or offend your loved one or someone else.

> *"It is not a lack of love, but a lack of friendship that makes unhappy marriages."*
> Friedrich Nietzsche

 **#78 Occasionally Hide Love Notes**

Periodically hide short love notes around the house where they will be found by your loved one (e.g., in the laundry basket, taped to a deodorant or shave cream can, in a carton of eggs, taped to a cereal box, in the medicine cabinet, or attached to a piece of clothing worn regularly).

 **#79 Record a Personal Message**

Record a personal message to your spouse or significant in which you share your feelings. For example, you might talk about memories you have with each other, how you feel about you loved one and why, what you like most about him or her and why, how much you enjoy activities together, or what you want to do with him or her when you meet again. When they travel, slip the thumb drive or memory card containing the message into an envelope along with a love note or greeting card containing a personal message and put it in their briefcase, suitcase or computer case for him or her to find later.

> *"We cannot really love anyone with whom we never laugh."*
> Agnes Repp

 **#80 Call to Sing on Special Occasions**

Call your loved one's cell phone and sing *Happy Birthday* or *Happy Anniversary* to him or her. If they do not answer leave a recorded song.

 **#81 Bake Customized Fortune Cookies**

The next time you order in or make Chinese food, bake customized fortune cookies with messages that you create to insert in each one. For a recipe, search the Internet or visit http://allrecipes.com/Recipe/Fortune-Cookies-So-Easy/.

 **#82 Program a Custom Desktop Background Image**

When your loved one is not around, right click on his or her computer desktop area, select *Personalize,* select *Desktop Background* at the bottom of the screen, browse to select a customized photo with text that you have created, then save the image. It will automatically display when the computer is turned on. This might be a favorite photo of you and your loved one with text that says "*(your name) Loves (your loved one's name).*" To create this image, go to PowerPoint or some other slide program you use, import a photo and add text to a slide and save it as a JPEG file in your computer photo library. Next, proceed as mentioned above.

 **#83 Hide a Piece of Jewelry**

Purchase a special piece of jewelry and present it to your loved one inside a box of candy. Just make sure its presence is obvious; dental work can be expensive!

"True love cannot be found where it does not exist, nor can it be denied where it does."
Torquato Tasso

#84 Plaster the House with Love Notes

Use an entire pad of Sticky Notes to create love messages. Post these notes all over the house where they are likely to be seen (e.g., refrigerator, exit and entrance doors, sink, toilet seat, mirrors, kitchen cabinets, and television and computer screens) Sample messages include:

- *I Love You!*
- *You are the greatest spouse!*
- *Life with you is awesome!*
- *Thank you for loving me.*
- *I am SO glad you are in my life!*
- *You are the greatest parent!*
- *Loving you means everything to me!*
- *Life with you is fantastic!*
- *I am proud to be you wife/husband.*
- *If I could choose all over again, I'd choose YOU!*
- *You make my life complete!*
- *Loving you gives me purpose!*
- *I want to spend the rest of my life with YOU!*
- *Thank you for being my best friend.*

Tap The Element Of Surprise

"You don't love someone because they're perfect, you love them in spite of the fact that they're not."
Jodi Picoult

 **Write "I Love You" on a Piece of Fruit**

Use a marker to write *I Love You* on an orange or banana that your partner will be eating for breakfast or a snack.

 Place a Gift on the Pillow

Just as hotels often do, place a small memento (e.g., candy or a flower) of appreciation on your loved one's pillow. Perhaps couple this with one of the gift certificates mentioned elsewhere in this book for a night of sensuous pleasure, a massage or some other fun treat.

 **Celebrate with a Cupcake**

Surprise your loved one with a cupcake and candle following dinner on a special date (e.g., the date you first met, your first date, the purchase of your first house or car, birth of a child, a promotion or getting a new job). Depending on the event, you might also give her or him a present as well.

 **Have Flowers Delivered**

Have a dozen roses or other favorite flowers delivered to your loved one for no special reason. You could also arrange to take your loved one out to a romantic dinner the night the flowers arrive. Remember that many men like flowers too!

#89 Prepare a Special Homecoming

When your loved one comes home from a trip or work, greet him or her at the door with a big kiss and smile and wearing a bathrobe with nothing under it!

#90 Hire a Limousine

If you can afford to do so, hire a limousine for transportation to surprise your loved one on a special occasion. For example, an anniversary, birthday, awards banquet, departure on your honeymoon or special trip, or whenever you just want to surprise and treat your loved one special and add a new memory to the occasion.

#91 Put a Note in a Balloon

Write a short love note and place it inside a balloon. Write *POP ME* on the outside of the balloon with a marker. Put the balloon inside your loved one's car or somewhere in the house where it will be readily found. An alternative could be to put a ticket for a special event or trip inside the balloon.

"You know it is love when forever is not long enough."
Unknown

Tap The Element Of Surprise

 **#92 Mail a Giant Greeting Card**

Many gift and card stores sell huge greeting cards for special occasions (e.g., Valentine's Day, birthdays, or Christmas). Get one of these and write a personal message of love inside or include a handwritten letter. Send it to your loved one.

 **#93 Throw a Surprise Party**

Throw a surprise party and invite friends and family to help celebrate special occasions, such as your loved one's birthday, promotion, academic or professional achievement or new job.

 **#94 Hide a Love Letter**

If your spouse or significant other is going on a trip, slip a love letter into their suitcase where they will find it upon arrival at their destination. Include a gift certificate for an intimate evening when they return to give her or him something to look forward to.

"Falling in love and having a relationship are two different things."

Keanu Reeves

STRENGTHEN THE COMMUNICATION FLOW

 **#95 Be Considerate of Your Loved One**

In relationships, each partner must consider the feelings and needs of the other. Before accepting invitations from other people, making a decision that affects you both, or doing other things that involves your loved one, make sure to check with him or her first in order to get their input before committing to something. For all you know, your loved one may have planned a surprise getaway for the two of you. Your failure to plan together may create dissatisfaction and may even cause your partner to be reluctant to try to plan future surprises for you.

"The relationship between husband and wife should be one of best friends."
B.R. Ambedkar

 **#96 Celebrate Your Love**

Life is short. Learn to communicate effectively, work together on activities and take every opportunity to find ways to build new memories and show your love.

 **#97 Attend Communication Classes**

Take time out of your schedule to attend local or Internet classes or webinars on gender and interpersonal communication in order to hone the key skills needed for a successful relationship. Take your loved one along so that he or she can also gain new insights and work with you to improve your relationship.

 **#98 Never Go To Bed Angry**

When a disagreement occurs, take the time to calmly talk out the causes and come to an acceptable resolution. Ideally, this discussion should not occur in the bedroom. Go to a neutral room.

By all means, make sure that you focus on the behavior that led to the disagreement and avoid name calling or focusing on your loved one. For example, you should never attack the person with language like "You are an idiot" or "You're ALWAYS or NEVER doing . . . ." Such words degrade your loved one and escalate emotions. In reality, in such instances, if he or she can offer one instance where they did not do something for which you have accused her or him, your argument is null and void because they have then demonstrated that they do not "always" or "never" do something. Many people forget this simple communication technique and use words that wound and cause rifts in the relationship. They might even bring up past issues or unresolved points if those have not been sufficiently handled in the past. These are all recipes for damage to a relationship.

Strengthen The Communication Flow

"The best love is the one person that makes you a better person without changing you into someone other than yourself."

Unknown

 **#99 Start a Nightly Tradition**

Make an agreement with your spouse or significant other that, before you each say *I love you,* kiss and go to sleep, that you will share one thing that you each appreciated the other doing during that day. It is okay to repeat things throughout the year, just don't use the same actions every night.

Some examples follow:

- *Getting the kids ready for school.*
- *Putting the dirty laundry in the washer before leaving for work.*
- *Brewing coffee in the morning.*
- *Emptying the dishwasher.*
- *Bringing in the newspaper.*
- *Hugging and kissing when they came home from work.*
- *Stopping to pick up items from the grocery store or the dry cleaners.*

"Love is a canvas provided by nature and embroidered by imagination."

Voltaire

# #100 Call to Say I Love You

Make it a habit of calling your spouse or significant other on any given day to express your love and ask how their day is going. This helps you stay involved in their professional life, know what they are working on and shares your love for her or him. An alternative to this strategy is to text or email your loved one. Just remember that person-to-person is always a more powerful way to connect since your loved one likely gets dozens of written messages a day and yours might get lost in the shuffle.

# #101 Use the Word "Please" in Requests

People who spend time in relationships sometimes get lazy and start making their requests into statements or demands by omitting the simple word *please*. Consciously include this word when you ask your loved one to do get or do something for you. For example, "Will you please bring me another drink?" or "Please turn off the kitchen light." Little acts of courtesy are often recognized and appreciated.

# #102 Say the Words "I Love You"

Lovers, family and friends say "I love you." It has been said that sincerely using these three simple words can help build and strengthen any personal relationship if both parties share the sentiment. Even so, many couples fail to remember the importance of this simple phrase on any given day. While they may think warmly about their partner and about expressing their love, they often fail to regularly use the words. This can lead to feelings of self-doubt or doubt in a partner and can ultimately lead to a weakening or breakdown in the relationship and potentially infidelity. People who do not feel loved at home often seek it elsewhere.

> *"If you love someone, tell them because hearts are often broken by words left unspoken."*
> Unknown

 **#103 Write a Love Letter**

Send a love letter via the postal service. Love letters have traditionally been a means of professing one's feelings for centuries. Unfortunately, with the advent of technology, a lot of people fail to use this vehicle of communication too often. For that reason, it could have an unexpected impact when your spouse or significant other receives an unexpected letter in the mail from you.

To prepare it, spend some thoughtful time thinking of your innermost feelings for your partner. Share such things as why your loved one is special, the qualities which they demonstrate that you like, what first attracted you, how they make you feel, the things you like about your relationship, or whatever comes to mind. If you are a woman, use the old technique of spraying a bit of your favorite perfume on the letter and sealing the envelope with a lipstick impression of your kiss.

> *"When you truly love someone,
> no matter what happens and
> no matter what mistakes get made,
> you never give up the fight to make things right."*
> Unknown

 **#104 Discuss Daily Events**

Spend time at meals or other appropriate moments discussing daily occurrences (e.g., what happened at work or local and world events). This can enhance communication and provide insights into what is important to each of you and how you both feel about life and the things going on around the world. Open communication also demonstrates an interest on your part to share and hear your loved one's perspectives and can often help strengthen your relationship.

 **#105 Create a Secret Nonverbal Message**

Come up with a secret nonverbal signal that the two of you use regularly from a distance to say *I Love You*. It might be something as simple as pointing to your eye, followed by crossing your arms to signify a hug (love), then pointing at your loved one to say *I (eye) Love You.*

> *"Forgiveness is the final form of love."*
> Reinhold Niebuhr

Strengthen The Communication Flow

 **#106 Communicate Openly**

Many people, especially men, are often reluctant to share their true feelings, especially in emotional situations. In many families and societies men are taught to be stoic, masculine and not to cry. Likewise, many women hesitate to share their emotions because they do not want to be perceived as the weaker sex, especially in workplace situations. This behavior sometimes carries over into home life.

In the proper time, place and situation, it is normal and appropriate to share what is on your mind or your true feelings with your loved one. In fact, research shows that allowing the emotions to spill out and having someone listen empathetically is a very cathartic remedy for easing pain or distress. In some instances, your reluctance to open up and share your emotions in stressful situations might be viewed as a lack of trust by your partner. This could potentially damage your relationship in the long term.

 **#107 Call When You Are Going to Be Late**

Sometimes unexpected events can cause delays in life. You would likely call a business contact to notify of delays and apologize if you were going to be late for a meeting, so why not provide the same courtesy to the person you love. Such behavior shows respect and appreciation especially if you inconvenience your loved one (e.g., you are late for a meal or event that they have taken time to prepare or plan for).

 **#108 Communicate During Sex**

Discuss how your partner feels about talking during sex. In many instances sharing your thoughts, feelings, fantasies wishes can enhance the experience for both partners. Use whatever words or language you both prefer. Talking dirty sometimes gets a bad rap. See *Resources for Lovers* in the back of this book for ideas on this topic.

> *"We love the things we love for what they are."*
> Robert Frost

 **#109 Prepare a Relationship Questionnaire**

Pretend that someday you will both be on a game show similar to the *Newlywed Game* in which participants are asked questions and predict how their loved one will answer. Create a series of questions that will help you get to know more about your spouse or significant other. End each question with *Why?* In order to better understand your loved one's motivations or reasoning process. You might choose some of the questions from the book *4,000 Questions for Getting to Know Anyone and Everyone* in the *Resources for Lovers* section of this book.

Some question possibilities include:

- *What is your favorite color? Why?*
- *What is your favorite season of the year? Why?*
- *If you could travel anywhere in the world, where would you go? Why?*

Strengthen The Communication Flow

- *If you could change one thing about yourself, what would it be? Why?*
- *If you could change one thing about me, what would it be? Why?*
- *What do you like most about yourself? Why?*
- *What do you like least about yourself? Why?*
- *What do you like most about me? Why?*
- *What do you like least about me? Why?*

"Real intimacy is only possible to the degree that we can be honest about what we are doing and feeling."
Dr. Joyce Brothers

#110 Establish a (VoIP) Account

Make sure that your technology has a camera component so that you can set up and use a free Skype or similar video conferencing or Voice Over Internet Protocol (VoIP) account in order to stay in touch and see one another each time either of you travels. These technologies allow inexpensive voice and video communication via wireless Internet connections.

#111 Acknowledge When You Are Wrong

Most people appreciate the feeling that they were correct during a discussion or argument. By simply saying "You are right" during a conversation when you said or did something that was incorrect you can potentially diffuse anger and resentment and empower your loved one.

RECAPTURE PASSION AND SENSUALITY

*"You're lucky if you have someone
who always tries to understand you,
your anger, mistakes, stupid decisions
and never gets tired of it."*
Tinku Razoria

 **#112 Use Love Touches**

Physical touch can be a way of showing your spouse or significant other that you love, care and value him or her as a person and as a partner. Tactile contact with your spouse or significant other can non-verbally send messages of liking, love, or desire. When these touches are accompanied by words such as *I love you,* your nonverbal message is strengthened.

Depending on the personality style and the situation or location in which you and your spouse or significant other is located, you can send powerful subtle messages through touch.

Some common means of demonstrating affection in this manner include:

- *A hug and kiss as you pass each other in the house or when you come into a room where they are located.*

- *A kiss on forehead or on the back or side of their neck from behind while they are seated.*

- *Stroking the back of the neck or side of their face as you drive.*
- *Playfully scratching their back or massaging shoulders from behind.*
- *Holding hands.*
- *Massaging your partner's hands, back, neck, and feet as you watch television.*

 **#113 Play Strip Poker or Other Card Game**

Spend the evening with your loved one playing strip poker, rummy, or other favorite game. When you lose a hand, you must cede an article of clothing. Once all clothing is gone, you can think of something else to do!

 **#114 Plan Regular Date Nights**

Keeping the relationship spark alive requires conscious effort. Make time for one another by scheduling at least one night a week to do something together. Take a bike ride or walk around the block to talk or a trip to a local fast-food restaurant. You might also take a bubble bath together and schedule a "play date" for intimacy. The important thing is that no matter how long you have been a couple; reconnect and share regularly.

"Where there is love there is life."
Mahatma Gandhi

 **#115 Watch Romantic, Sensual Movies**

Indulge your fantasies and add a bit of excitement by choosing a sensual X-rated movie that you believe you will both enjoy and watch it together.

 **#116 Let Your Loved One Orchestrate Sex**

Instead of defaulting to your normal sexual routine, allow your partner to make the decision based on his/her preference for an evening of romance.

 **#117 Make Love in Front of a Fireplace**

Add a figurative spark to your relationship and have a spontaneous lovemaking session in front of a roaring fire. If you do not have a fireplace, you can buy computer software that can be hooked up to your television that imitates a fireplace. Add in a bottle of your favorite wine or other drink and you have the makings of a private party.

 **#118 Fall Asleep Spooning**

Make your last conscious moment of the day a memory of having your loved one wrapped around you (or you around him or her) as you drift off to sleep holding hands.

"Love is an emotion experienced by many and enjoyed by few."
George Jean Nathan

 **#119 Be Uninhibited Around Your Partner**

Make sure the blinds are closed in your home and then act spontaneously around your loved one. Go naked, have spontaneous sex, surprise her or him by joining in a shower, or let your mind run wild. If you are naturally shy, work to be more uninhibited in private around your partner. Talk about your reluctance and discuss ways to overcome it.

 **#120 Share our Inner Feelings and Fantasies**

For many reasons, some people are reluctant to share their inner thoughts and fantasies with their loved one. Open up with your spouse or significant other. You may be surprised to find they share your feelings or perspectives and you never know where that might lead you both. Check out the *Resources for Lovers* section at the end of this book for ideas.

"Treasure your relationships, not your possessions."
Anthony J. D'Angelo

 **#121 Use Passionate Kisses Freely**

Remember when you first met and those kisses with your loved one seemed to last forever? Why not recapture those memories and make new ones by spending time recreating the passion of earlier days.

 **#122 Be Spontaneously Intimate**

Many couples let other life activities take control of their lives and settle into a routine. They often seem to have little time for intimacy with the one they care about the most in life. This can damage a relationship over time. Strive to bring back the spark and focus on your loved one by being more spontaneous when it comes to intimacy.

 **#123 Have Phone Sex**

When your loved one travels on business; call to have phone sex in the evening. Build a bit of fantasy into the call by adapting your voice to sound seductious, ask for your spouse by Mr. or Ms. ____ when they answer and tell him or her that you are calling as a present from their loved one. Then proceed to talk provocatively to your sweetheart. See the *Resources for Lovers* section in the back of this book for role play suggestions.

> *"You can give without loving,*
> *but you can never love without giving."*
> Robert Louis Stevenson

 **#124 Prepare a "Love String"**

Start at the entrance to your house or apartment and tape a long string from room to room leading to the bedroom. Along the way, tape small notes with a couple of words of a message to your loved one at different intervals along the way. By the time he or she gets to the bedroom, after having read the entire message, you'll be waiting in the bedroom or bath tub with their favorite drink. For example, you might have a message like, "Follow this string for a well-earned surprise . . . Throughout our relationship, I have always gotten excited and smiled when I knew you were on your way home to me. You are my everything. I cherish each day of our relationship and each moment that I spend with you. I cannot wait to see you again!"

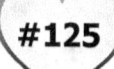

#125   Take a Bubble Bath or Shower Together

Spend some time in a bubble bath or shower together, wash one another's back, get back in touch with the excitement you may have experienced when your relationship was new. If you never experienced that pleasure, give it a try to add new spark to your lives. If you are in a tub, share a bottle of wine, add some fragranced candles around the tub, and play some romantic music. Just enjoy the moment; talk or caress one another.

#126   Take an Idea Excursion

Wander around an adults only store with your loved one some afternoon. Look at items displayed there and discuss which ones you might like to bring home to try out.

> *"There is no love without forgiveness and no forgiveness without love."*
> Bryant H. McGill

#127  Spin for Sex

Buy a numbered game spinner (e.g., On eBay, Amazon and other Internet site) and a copy of the *Kama Sutra* listed in the *Resources for Lovers* section at the back of this book. Assign corresponding numbers to the positions in the book, spin and try whatever is indicated. This is a fun way to add a spark back into your life.

#128  Plan an Intimate Evening

Take the time to plan an intimate evening to surprise your loved one. This might include a bubble bath or special meal, followed by an evening complete with scented candles, low lights, romantic music, and a massage.

#129  Request a Play Date

Text, email or leave a voice message for your loved one requesting a *play date* where you will meet in the bedroom to mutually satisfy one another.

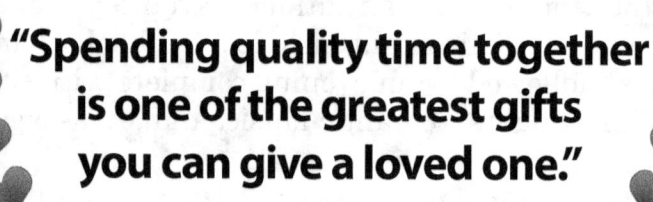

"Spending quality time together is one of the greatest gifts you can give a loved one."

Robert W. Lucas

REINFORCE CARING AND SECURITY

 **#130 Remember Special Dates**

Most people who have forgotten a special date (e.g., birthday, anniversary, Valentines, Mother's or Father's Day) normally make a concerted effort not to let that omission occur again after they realize the impact on their loved one. With the advent of technology, all the reminders in online calendars, and with traditional calendars, there is little reason to forget a special date. To ensure serenity in your relationship, put special dates on your calendar(s) and have a backup plan not to forget!

> *"Let us always meet each other with a smile, for the smile is the beginning of love."*
> Mother Teresa

 **#131 Plan for a Financial Crisis**

One of the biggest mistakes that many couples make is that they fail to think about and plan for potential catastrophes, such as, death or incapacitation of a loved one. One of the easiest ways to reduce stress on your partner and show your love is to consult a lawyer and accountant and consider at least the following actions in advance, if appropriate:

- *Create a will and living will.*

- *Set up a power of attorney.*
- *Pre-plan funeral arrangements*
- *Set up a "transfer upon death" form listing your loved one on checking and savings accounts, retirement funds, and other finance-related accounts.*
- *Arrange for joint right of ownership for all property (e.g., houses, land, boat, and vehicles).*
- *Set up a trust (depending on your assets), if a lawyer agrees.*
- *Put all important papers (e.g., insurance papers, wills, living wills, financial documents, contracts, retirement fund information) in a safe and ensure they know how to open it. Also have backup copies kept in a safe location off-site.*
- *Discuss plans for dealing with various legal, medical, and personal crises.*
- *Keep a current list of all recurring bills, security password for technology, financial institutions and account numbers, or other critical information. Keep this with your important documents and make sure your loved one knows about it.*

"The highest function of love is that it makes the loved one a unique and irreplaceable being."
Tom Robbins

 #132 Demonstrate Your Love in Small Ways

There are so many small things that you can do to say (e.g., "You are special and I love you") to your spouse or significant other to show that you care. You are limited only by your imagination and willingness to put forth the effort to make your loved one happy and feel special.

Some potential strategies to demonstrate love follow:

- *Serve your partner breakfast in bed or cook a special dish for lunch or dinner. If cooking is not one of your strengths or you prefer to go out, take your partner to a nice restaurant.*

- *Plant a tree or perennial flower bush (one that returns each year) for your loved one on the date of some special occasion (e.g., anniversary when you met or got married, or the birth or adoption of a child or animal).*

- *Share a bubble bath together.*

- *Spell "I Love You" in shave cream on the bathroom counter.*

- *Be positive about life around your loved one at every opportunity.*

- *Open a door or pull out a chair for your mate or let him or her precede you through a doorway.*

- *Buy a small present for no particular reason. This might include such things as tickets to a show or movie your spouse wants to see, gift certificate for a massage or personal grooming visit, or flowers.*

- *Bring home a box of candy with a card for special occasions or for no reason at all.*
- *Detail your loved one's car without being asked.*
- *Buy her a silk nightgown or him a pair of silk pajamas or boxer shorts.*
- *Propose in an unusual and romantic manner.*
- *Prepare a candlelit dinner with his or her favorite food and use your best china.*

"The things that we truly love stay with us always, locked away in our hearts as long as life remains."
Josephine Baker

#133 Sign Up for a Road Service Membership

To ensure that you and your loved one are safe when traveling, sign up for OnStar, AAA, AARP, or other roadside assistance memberships. Many car insurance policies offer these at lower prices, but without all the added benefits of a traditional travel group plan.

#134 Sign Up for a CPR Class Together

You never know when a medical emergency is going to occur where CPR could mean the difference between life and death for you or your loved one. Ask your spouse or significant other to register for a local CPR training class with you to learn this important skill.

Reinforce Caring And Security

*"Love is needing someone.
Love is putting up with someone's bad qualities
because they somehow complete you."*
Sarah Dessen

 **#135 Kiss Your Loved One's Hand**

As you drive down the road or are seated in a theatre, restaurant, on the sofa or wherever, spontaneously draw your loved ones hand to you and kiss it while making eye contact and expressing your love or feelings for her or him.

 **#136 Allow Your Partner to Choose a Seat**

Many people have preferred seats on airplanes, in restaurants, on public transportation and in other venues. Allow your partner to make their selection first (e.g., window seat on an airplane or facing into a restaurant) occasionally, even if you'd prefer that location. Little gestures such as this can send a message of caring or consideration for another person.

 **#137 Bring Flowers To Your Loved One**

If your spouse or significant other becomes ill and cannot leave the house or is hospitalized for several days, bring greeting cards, love notes, flowers, balloons or other surprise items each time you come to visit or come home from work. These little gestures can often help cheer someone up. Because of over-familiarity, people in long-term relationships often do not think that to take simple actions like these, even though they would likely afford such offerings to friends or family members in similar circumstances.

#138 Share the Remote Control

It is amazing that something as simple as placing the television remote control on the opposite side of yourself from where your partner is sitting can send a subliminal message that you are controlling or inconsiderate. Learn to consciously share it, and other things, in your relationship.

#139 Leave the Last Item

One of the simplest ways to show that you love and care for your spouse or significant other is to never take the last item in a package (e.g., cookie, fruit, drink, or other item). Leave that for your loved one with a small note stating that "I left this for you . . . I Love You that much!"

MAXIMIZE TIME SPENT TOGETHER

 **#140 Go for a Nature Walk Together**

Visit local parks and forests to take a stroll through nature with your loved one as you hold hands, talk, and make future plans. Take photos top reinforce your memories.

"Love is composed of a single soul inhabiting two bodies."
Aristotle

 **#141 Take an Evening Stroll**

When the weather is nice, go for a walk with your loved one under the stars after dinner. Talk about life issues and feelings as you plan and discuss things that you may not have time for otherwise. Hold hands as you walk. Not only does this help to potentially solidify your relationship; it is also good for your health.

 **#142 Take Lessons Together**

To give you both something else in common and that you can do together, check local colleges, the YMCA, social clubs, library, museums, or other resources for classes that you can take to learn a new skill or enhance knowledge. For example, SCUBA diving, horseback riding, canoeing, dancing, local history sessions, art appreciation, sky diving or other fun activity that you might both enjoy.

 ### #143 Watch the Sunset over the Ocean or a Lake

For no special reason, take a trip to the beach, a lake or park to watch the sunset with your loved one. If permitted at the location, take a bottle of wine and toast to your love as the sun goes down. Seal the moment with a kiss and a promise to love eternally.

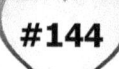 ### #144 Buy a Bicycle Built for Two

Have some fun and get some exercise at the same time by getting a bicycle built for two and going for regular rides with your loved one.

> *"You never lose by loving.*
> *You always loseby holding back."*
> Barbara de Angelis

 ### #145 Go for a Canoe or Rowboat Ride

There is something about being out on a lake or slow moving river in a canoe or row boat with your loved one that blocks out the rest of the world while allowing you to build a lasting memory.

Maximize Time Spent Together

#146 Go on a Nighttime Picnic

Find a scenic location in your area where you have access to the stars without a lot of bothersome street or housing lighting. Spread a blanket on the ground, take out a picnic basket with wine, cheese or other snacks and drinks and spend the evening talking and gazing up at the stars. If the location and mood is right, make love under the open sky.

#147 Select a Pet Together

Go to a local pet adoption agency or SPCA to find an abandoned animal to become part of your family. Most people find that these loving creatures bring warmth and continuity to the home as both partners care for and learn to love the new pet as part of the family.

#148 Make Hot Chocolate on a Cold Day

Prepare a tray with hot chocolate and treats to share with your spouse or significant other on a patio or in front of a television on a cold or damp day. If you are outside, bring along a blanket or throw to wrap around you both as you enjoy your drinks, cuddle and talk to one another.

> *"We can grow our relationships with others by leaps and bounds if we become encouragers instead of critics."*
> Joyce Meyer

 **#149 Take a Hay Ride**

Many farms and non-profit groups (e.g., religious organizations, American Legions, Boy/Girl Scouts) sell pumpkins for Halloween during the month of October to raise funds. They also offer hay rides on the back of trailers pulled by tractors or horses. Search for one of these events in your local area and plan to take a ride with your loved one where you can hold hands and have photos of the two of you taken as you enjoy the event together and build more memories.

 **#150 Carve a Jack O' Lantern Together**

Have a bit of fun at Halloween and work with your spouse or significant other to carve jack o' lanterns with different faces, hearts, or the word *LOVE*.

"No partner in a love relationship ... should feel that he has to give up an essential part of himself to make it viable."

May Sarton

 **#151 Suggest a Formal Date Night**

Don't wait for a special occasion to get dressed up in fine clothing to go to dinner. Suggest that you both put on your best attire and go to a nice restaurant where you spend the evening talking, holding hands, and looking into one another's eyes.

 **#152 Attend an Arts and Crafts Festival**

Spend a weekend with your loved one wandering through local art or craft festivals, flea markets or other such venues. Enjoy the weather and one another's company, have a casual lunch and maybe later a nice dinner for just the two of you.

 **#153 Watch Home Movies Together**

When was the last time you brought out old home movies and watched these with your spouse or significant other? Rekindle old personal family memories. Make some popcorn and start the show. If the movies are from times prior to your relationship, they might also help you learn more about each other. A conversation to gain new insights could likely follow as a result.

 **#154 Play "What If"**

Use the game of *What If* to dream as a couple and discover how you each feel about a variety of topics. For example:

- *What if we won the lottery tomorrow . . . what would we do first?*
- *What if we could go anywhere in the world . . . where would it be?*
- *What if we had three wishes . . . what would they be?*
- *What if money were no object . . . what would you buy?*

- *What if you could change one thing about me . . . what would that be?*
- *What if we could build a new house tomorrow . . . what would it look like inside and out?*

> **"If there is such a thing as a good marriage, it is because it resembles friendship rather than love."**
> Michel de Montaigne

#155 Print a Photo Jigsaw Puzzle

Many photo labs and print shops can now turn your favorite photographs into a custom printed jigsaw puzzle. Choose one of your favorite personal images and have a jigsaw puzzle made as a gift for your loved one. Put it together as a couple.

#156 Dress Alike on Halloween

If you go to a costume party or take the kids trick or treating, wear matching costumes.

#157 Plan a Get-Away

Whether it is at a local facility or something more distant, taking the time to get away from your normal routine can often rekindle romance and help you reconnect with your loved one. Depending on your finances, you might reserve a bed and breakfast or resort or schedule an extended getaway to a more distant location.

Maximize Time Spent Together

*"It is not how much we have,
but how much we enjoy that makes happiness."*
Charles Spurgeon

 **#158 Watch a Romantic Movie Together**

Fix some popcorn and turn on a romantic movie for just the two of you to watch. Hold hands and snuggle to really get the most out of the experience. Movies like *When Harry Met Sally* or *Sleepless in Seattle* are classics.

 **#159 Dedicate a Song on the Radio**

If your loved one listens to a particular radio station and the DJ takes phone dedications, call in to request a special song. If your loved one is not available when the song is played, record it and share later when you are together or connected via Internet.

 **#160 Express Your Love on a Button**

The next time you pass a vendor making customized lapel buttons, have pins created for both you and your loved one that declares *This is what love looks like* or *I Love (your loved one's name)*. Wear these proudly as you walk through the mall or other public place! You can do the same thing with a baseball cap, t-shirt, coffee mug or other similar product.

*"There is only one happiness in this life,
to love and be loved."*
George Sand

 **#161 Plan a Picnic**

When was the last time you were on a picnic with your loved one? Find a scenic location in your area, pick up a nice bottle of wine or other drinks that you both like, download some romantic songs to your smart phone or recording device, pack or buy food items and put these items in a basket or cooler (don't forget the condiments and eating utensils, plates, napkins and other appropriate items), and then head off with your loved one to enjoy a day together.

 **#162 Go Horseback Riding**

Search the Internet for riding trails in your area, call and make reservations and then surprise your loved one with a unique and fun riding event. If you cruise or travel internationally, there are numerous locations around the world where you can find riding opportunities on beaches or in rural areas. What a memorable way to remember a trip! Don't forget photos of the two of you on horseback. They make a great jigsaw puzzle.

 **#163 Make S'mores Together**

Enjoy an evening in front of a backyard fire pit making s'mores and just talking.

 **#164 Have a Barbeque**

If you do not often barbeque, cook steaks or other favorite foods on the backyard grill and share with your loved one along with a nice bottle of wine. Follow this with an evening watching whatever movie your loved one chooses as you hold hands or cuddle.

> *"For the two of us, home isn't a place. It's a person. And we are finally home."*
> Stephanie Perkins

 **Put a Jigsaw Puzzle Together**

Buy a jigsaw puzzle with an image of some special place you have visited and spend an evening putting it together with your loved one. Many gift stores in tourist locations sell such items. Pop open a bottle of wine or get some other favorite drinks and make some popcorn to make the evening more fun.

 **Take a Hot Air Balloon Ride Together**

Attend the Albuquerque International Balloon Fiesta in October and ride a hot air balloon. The event is world renowned and thousands of hot air balloon enthusiasts participate each year in a visual panorama of color and excitement as hundreds of balloons rise simultaneously into the sky. If you cannot make this event, there are smaller events across the U.S. and overseas.

 **Plan a Game Night**

Make plans with your loved one to play cards or a board/electronic game with him or her. Use the time together to talk about whatever topic comes to mind.

 **#168 Have Fun Together**

Life is too short not to have fun. Take the time to enjoy opportunities to have fun together. Some instances might be:

- *Build a snowman.*
- *Shovel snow together and have a snowball fight.*
- *Go for a swim in a local river, at the beach or in your own pool.*
- *Build a fire in the fireplace or in a fire pit and sit next to it as you talk.*
- *Roast marshmallows and make s'mores.*
- *Open a bottle of wine and watch television together.*
- *Jump into a Fall leaf pile together and wrestle.*
- *Fall asleep as you "spoon" or cuddle one another.*
- *Have a pillow fight.*
- *Bake something or cook a special meal together.*

 #169 Take on a Volunteer Project

Work as partners on a volunteer project in which you help others and give back to your community or society in some manner. Possible ventures might include:

- *Participating in a fundraising run for the Cancer or Heart Associations.*
- *Delivering meals to senior or disabled persons.*
- *Helping build a Habitat House*
- *Signing up to be a Big Brother/Big Sister.*
- *Working at a homeless shelter.*
- *Ringing a bell for the Salvation Army during the holidays.*
- *Being a youth mentor for your religious organization.*

In any of these instances, you are forming new memories and building potential subjects of conversation while providing valuable services and assisting those who need help.

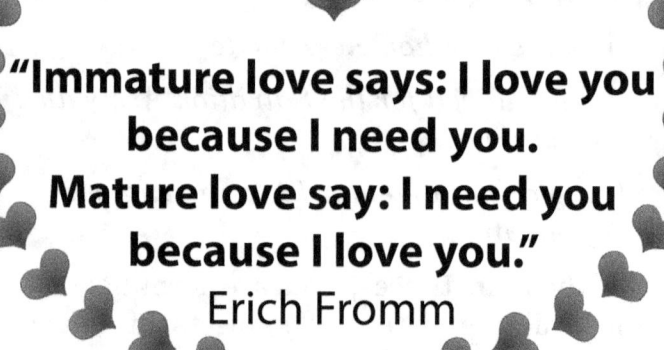

"Immature love says: I love you because I need you.
Mature love say: I need you because I love you."
Erich Fromm

CAPITALIZE ON SPONTANEITY

 **Openly Flirt with Your Loved One**

It is better that you should flirt with your loved one, rather than having someone else do so. Be spontaneous with some playful flirting and appropriate touching when out with friends or when the two of you are on a date night. These little actions can reinforce that you still find your mate desirable and attractive and that you love him or her.

"Being deeply loved by someone gives you strength, while loving someone deeply gives you courage."

Lao Tzu

 **Do the Unexpected**

To add a bit of spark to your relationship, do something unexpected that your loved one knows you would not normally do. For example, take your spouse or significant other to a theme park or carnival and ride a roller coaster, bungee jump, or go roller skating or dancing.

#172 Act Like Newlyweds

Even if you have been together for years, you do not have to act like "an old married couple." Keep the spark alive in your relationship by regularly holding hands, gazing into one another's eyes, kissing spontaneously, telling your partner you love him or her numerous times throughout the day, and doing other things that you likely did when you first started out as a couple.

#173 Do Something Special

Occasionally make an effort to do something special for your loved one. This might be:

- *Driving to get a special flavor of coffee or ice cream not sold locally.*
- *Buying something that your loved one indicated he or she would like to have.*
- *Ordering a special carry out meal at a restaurant that your spouse or significant other enjoys.*
- *Picking up your loved one's clothes at the dry cleaners because he or she is too busy to do it.*
- *Taking the car in for an oil change or other maintenance work while your loved one uses your car for the day.*

"Passion is momentary; love is enduring."
John Wooden

#174 Plan an Impromptu Meal Together

If you are near your loved one's place of employment and both schedules permit, call to arrange a spur-of-the-moment lunch or dinner together.

Capitalize On Spontaneity

 **#175 Go for a Horse Drawn Carriage Ride**

Many cities in the U.S. and abroad offer horse drawn carriage rides. If you are in a location where this is available, take an evening ride as you cuddle and hold hands with your loved one.

 **#176 Buy or Bake an I Love You Cookie**

Either go to a local bakery or bake your own giant cookie and decorate it with the phrase "I Love You" or some other special message. Give it spontaneously or in celebration of some special occasion or event.

#177 Say I Love You with Flowers

If you have a flower bed in your yard, pick fresh flowers and put these in a vase by your partner's bedside, on the bathroom sink or dining table, along with a brief note declaring your love, a love poem, or a greeting card. Both men and women will likely enjoy this spontaneous gesture.

"Great love and great achievements involve great risk."
Unknown

 **#178 Dedicate a Song**

If you are at a bar, piano bar, on a cruise or in other venues with a live band or DJ, dedicate a special song to your loved one.

#179 Hold Hands When Walking

Reach out and spontaneously take your partner's hand as you walk along a street. Tell him or her that you love him or her and share one of their traits that you really like as you walk

#180 Stop and Pick Wildflowers

When traveling by car, spontaneously stop by the roadside and pick a wildflower or take a photo of it for your loved one. If you do the latter, get a print of the image made when you return home and frame it as a memory of your excursion.

> *"The way to love is to realize that it may be lost."*
> Gilbert K. Chesterton

#181 Buy a Spontaneous Present

When you are out with your loved one while on a trip, at the mall, a restaurant or other places where small gifts are available, buy a gift for no special reason other than because you love him or her. When you give the item, make eye contact, smile, and tell your significant other that you love him or her and how special he or she is to you.

Possible gifts include:
- *A flower (for a man or woman)*
- *Candy*

- *A garment (e.g., baseball cap, scarf, shirt, or other product you think they might wear or like)*
- *Jewelry*
- *Music*
- *Book or magazine*
- *Item to add to a collection that they have*

 **#182 Give a Special Occasion Gift Certificate**

A variation of the Gift Certificate of Love that you read about earlier is to create one that you give for special occasions like Mother's or Father's Day, Valentines, Christmas, birthdays, anniversaries, or other memorable events.

Make the certificate good for a day off from performing normal chores, such as, doing dishes, taking out the garbage, washing the dog, cleaning the litter box, cooking, cutting the lawn, cleaning the pool, washing and waxing the car or similar common tasks. On the day your loved one chooses, you or someone you hire can perform the task(s). Maybe even get your children involved to perform the task(s).

"Use things, not people. Love people, not things."
Unknown

 **#183 Buy a Balloon Heart**

Spontaneously have a balloon artist at a restaurant or on a street corner create a balloon heart for your loved one.

 **#184 Dance Spontaneously**

When a favorite song comes on the radio or is played at a social event, grab your partner and "dance like no one is watching!" Chances are that no one really is, so you can simply enjoy the spur-of-the-moment experience.

 **#185 Display Your Love on a Cold Day**

If you live in an area where snow or frost is common and you leave the house before your spouse or significant other, scrape the words *I Love You* and a heart on the windshield for your loved one to discover. Or, you could be nice and scrap the entire windshield clean and leave a love note under the wiper!

MAKE THE WORLD YOUR VEHICLE FOR LOVE

 **#186 Rent a Convertible Sports Car for Your Next Trip**

For a few dollars more than you might spend for a standard rental car, you can get a convertible for your next getaway with your loved one. Add a little zing to your getaway. Drive with the top down and sing songs together at the top of your voice while holding hands.

 **#187 Watch the New Year's Eve Ball Drop**

Either go to New York or watch the New Year's Eve celebration on television and count down the time as the ball drops. Celebrate with a big kiss and express your love for your partner as you gaze into your loved one's eyes.

> *"Never part without loving words to think of during your absence. It may be that you will not meet again in this life."*
> Jean Paul Richter

 **#188 Create a Travel Map**

Purchase a large framed map of the world and colored pins to use as a guide to where you have both traveled or desire to do so. Use three different colors for: (1) Places you have traveled individually, (2) Places you have visited together, and (3) Places that you want to visit together. In the latter case, once you have both traveled to a site, replace that pin with the second color indicating that you actually made a trip.

#189 Go for a Day Trip

If you are like most people with busy schedules, you probably have cities, towns or entertainment venues in your own state or country that are within a couple hours away which you keep saying you'd like to visit but never seem to get to. Take a weekend day or play hooky from work and take your loved one on a day trip. Enjoy yourself, build new memories and cross that location off of your "to do" list.

#190 Plan a Surprise Getaway

For special occasions, such as, the day you met, got engaged, first said "I love you," birthdays, or anniversaries, plan a special surprise getaway to a bed and breakfast, cruise, amusement park or whatever you both typically enjoy.

> *"The best love is the one person that makes you a better person without changing you into someone other than yourself."*
> Unknown

 **#191 Take a Trip to Las Vegas**

Las Vegas is a world unto its own, filled with energy, lots of people, and things to do twenty-four hours a day. You can get married or remarried in one of the many wedding chapels, visit casinos, go to various floor shows, shop or do whatever you choose. The advertising campaign that the city ran for years of "What happens in Vegas; Stays in Vegas" alludes to the opportunities awaiting you and your significant other. If you prefer not to spend all your time in one place, the Hoover Dam and Grand Canyon and many other scenic locations are within driving distance. Make the trip and some lasting memories at the same time.

 **#192 Visit a World Class City**

Take a trip to a world class city, like Washington DC, San Francisco, Paris, London, or New York. Once there, you and your loved one can explore all that it has to offer. For example, when visiting New York you might visit the Empire State Building, the Statue of Liberty and take a romantic carriage ride around Central Park.

"Love is but the discovery of ourselves in others, and the delight in the recognition."
Alexander Smith

 **#193 Kidnap Your Loved One**

Kidnap your loved one for a getaway weekend by preparing all the logistics, such as, reservations, childcare (if needed), packing a bag with clothes for both of you, toiletries, a scented candle, bottle of wine, recordings of your favorite music and other things that you would like to take along. Tell him or her at the last minute that you have a surprise weekend planned, get him or her in the car and head off on your love journey.

#194 Visit New Orleans

Plan a trip to this unique, romantic location and immerse

yourself in the food, dance and culture that will generate unforgettable memories for both you and your loved one. Stay in or near the French Quarter to get the full flavor of the area. For a special experience, go during Mardi Gras.

#195 Start a Trip Jar

Get a large pickle or other type jar and put a label that has the words *Trip Jar* taped to the outside. Discuss criteria for contributing with your spouse or significant other. For example, if either of you use a swear word, smoke a cigarette when you are trying to quit, fail to follow through on a promise, come home late from work, or whatever you think is important. Assign a dollar value to each infraction (e.g., $1.00 for swearing, $2.00 for smoking, and $3.00 for being late). Continue to add to the jar with each infraction and when you reach a specific set dollar amount, use the money for a weekend get-away or a vacation.

An alternative way to generate money in the jar is to drop in $5.00–$10.00 every time you make love. This is a win-win opportunity and might even inspire more intimacy in your relationship!

Make The World Your Vehicle For Love

"Love grows from stable relationships, shared experience, loyalty, devotion and trust."

Richard Wright

 **#196 Plan a Trip to Venice, Italy**

Use your Trip Jar money (discussed in #195) to take a trip to

Venice where you can ride a gondola while cuddling with your loved one. If you cannot afford a trip to Italy, fly to Las Vegas and stay, or make a stop, at the Venetian Hotel where they have real gondola rides.

"Marry a man/woman you love to talk to. As you get older, their conversational skills will be as important as any other."

Unknown

 **#197 Take a Cruise**

If you remember the television show *The Love Boat,* you might remember the power of cruising and falling in love or rekindling romance. There is something about traveling slowly on the seas to exotic locations that can add a spark to your relationship.

The great part about cruising is that they are one-stop escapes. Once you are aboard, you unpack and the crew does all the work. Your food, entertainment, and destinations are all included in the price. Depending on the time of year you travel and how far you live from a cruise port, these trips are really a bargain.

Contact Steve and Barbara Tanzer at TBSTravel (http://ourcruiseagent.com/) for a quality customer service experience.

#198 Eliminate a Bucket List Item

Many people have what is known as a "bucket list" of places

they want to go or things they want to do before they die. If you and your loved one have a list, commit to eliminating at least one item from the list on a regular basis (e.g., yearly). This can be fun and it can lead to new memories that you will both likely treasure for the rest of your life.

#199 Plan a Trip to a Romantic City

Discuss places that you would both like to go and select one that you both want to visit. This can be a local place in your region or anywhere else in the country or overseas. For example, San Francisco, Paris, Rome, the Grand Canyon, or whatever suits you both.

> *"When negative feelings are suppressed positive feelings become suppressed as well and love dies."*
> John Gray

#200 Subscribe to Travel Magazines

To get great ideas for travel destinations and escapes, subscribe or go to the library regularly to read prominent travel publications in print or online. See the *Resources for Lovers* section at the back of this book for more travel ideas.

GIVE THE GIFTS OF LOVE

#201 Gift a Car Detailing Certificate

Buy a gift certificate for a car detailing and wax at a local car wash facility. Give it to your loved one for any occasion.

#202 Declare "World's Greatest Lover"

Following a night of intimacy, put a "World's Greatest Lover" trophy on the bathroom sink area before your loved one gets up. You can buy these on the Internet and in some novelty stores or catalogs. If desired, you can also put a greeting card or note professing your love and appreciation with the trophy.

#203 Buy Etched Glasses

Have etched glasses made with special messages for use on special occasions (e.g., anniversaries, New Year's Eve, or birthdays). You can likely find vendors who etch glass in your local area or on the Internet.

> *"Never forget that the most powerful force on earth is love."*
> Nelson Rockefeller

 **#204 Make a Money Tree**

Go to a local nursery and purchase a small house tree (e.g., a Bonsai) to give to your loved one for a special occasion or whenever you feel like it. Hang various denominations of currency on the tree with paper clips and attached a card for the occasion that shares a love message that you want to send. Explain that the money is "mad money" to do with as your loved one desires.

 **#205 Give an Anniversary Ring**

Give your loved one a ring on a significant anniversary (e.g., fifth or twenty fifth). On such occasions, you might have a ring with one diamond for each year or five years of your relationship together or have a custom design created with whatever stones your loved one likes.

"You learn to speak by speaking, to study by studying, to run by running, to work by working; in just the same way, you learn to love by loving."

Anatole France

 **#206 Give a Heart-Shaped Paperweight**

Give a personalized heart-shaped paperweight to your loved one for his or her desk. You can find these online or in shops that personalize small gifts and have it engraved with a message or name and date.

 **#207 Give a Gift Certificate of Love**

There are many free templates for various types of gift certificates on the Internet. Search one of these out that has hearts or some other image you like on it and create a "Certificate of love." You can make the certificate for an intimate evening in your bedroom, a champagne bubble bath, a hot oil massage, a romantic dinner for two, or whatever you like. Let your imagination run wild!

 **#208 Have a Custom Quilt Made**

Find a local seamstress who can create a customized quilt with panels that reflect events in your life together. This type of gift can be a lasting representation of your life together and one that provides practical comfort on cold nights.

Cloth panels with various images are readily available on the Internet and in stores frequented by quilters.

Some possible quilt panels might include:

- *Baby to represent the birth of a child.*
- *Wedding cake topper image.*
- *African elephant to signify your safari together.*
- *Golf or other image, if one or both of you enjoy a specific sport.*
- *House to indicate your first home purchase.*
- *Large heart for the center of the quilt to represent your love for one another. Significant dates can be added to this.*

"The more one judges, the less one loves."
Honore de Balzac

 **#209 Send a Gift to Your Loved One**

If your spouse or significant other travels for business, have a fruit basket, tray of cookies or other treat sent to the hotel where he or she will be staying before they arrive. Contact the hotel and ask the front desk to have the gift waiting in your loved one's room when he or she checks in.

 **#210 Explore Your Genealogy**

Take the time to do a genealogy search of your family background and that of your loved one. Create a genealogy chart that you frame and give as a wedding, anniversary or birthday present. If you are not proficient in doing Internet research on your own or do not have the time, there are professional genealogists who will do this for a fee. What you create will be a lasting legacy for you and your loved one and for generations to come.

"Love makes your soul crawl out from its hiding place."
Zora Neale Hurston

 **#211 Fill the Car with Balloons**

When a significant milestone is reached (e.g., first day of a new job, promotion or graduation from college or a certification program) or on a special day (e.g., birthday or anniversary) go to your loved one's work parking lot and fill their car with helium balloons that have appropriate messages on each balloon (e.g., Happy Birthday/ Anniversary or Congratulations). Hide behind a tree with a camera to catch their reaction when they get off work.

 **#212 Purchase a Heart Umbrella**

Order an umbrella in the shape of a heart or with imprinted

hearts on it to keep your loved one dry in the rain. You can find these is some stores or on the Internet.

 **#213 Bring a Present When You Travel**

If you go away on a trip, bring your loved one a special gift when you return.

 **#214 Buy Puzzle Books**

If your loved one is a fan of puzzles (e.g., crossword, word search and Sudoku) buy books of these and give these as gifts on special occasions or whenever you like, along with a love note or greeting card. Wrap the gifts in heart covered paper.

 **#215 Give the Gift of Sensuality**

Give a gift certificate for Victoria's Secret or Frederick's of Hollywood. Go shopping together and choose sensual items that you both like.

"Love means to commit yourself without guarantee."
Anne Campbell

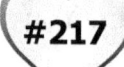 **#216 Give a Prepaid Gift or Charge Card**

Purchase a prepaid card and give it to your loved one in a greeting card that has a personal message from you. You can

give these for a special occasion or for no reason at all.

 **#217 Order a Customized Apron**

You can order customized aprons for the kitchen or barbeque with whatever message and image you desire through the Internet and in many kitchen and barbeque supply stores. Have one created for your loved one and give it on a special day or just because.

 **#218 Buy a Favorite Fragrance**

Go shopping and purchase a bottle of your loved one's favorite fragrance as a gift.

"If you can learn to love yourself and all the flaws, you can love other people so much better."
Kristin Chenoweth

#219 Give a Money Box as a Present

If you are stuck thinking of a present for a special event, crumple an equivalent of one hundred dollars in $1 and

$5 dollar bills (or as much as you would like to give) and put these in a wrapped box. Add a special greeting card for the occasion that has your written message stating how much you love him or her and that the money is to buy whatever he or she would like. Give this as a creative alternative to a gift card.

#220 Purchase a Collectable

If your loved one has a collection (e.g., post cards, animal characters, toys, or other things of sentimental value) look for an addition to the collection and give it to him or her for no special reason, or on a special day, along with a greeting card or note expressing your love.

#221 Bake Cookies or Special Treats

If your loved one enjoys sweet treats, bake some cookies, cupcakes, a pie or other goodies for no special reason. You might slip one of these into their lunch (if her or she takes one to work) along with an *I Love You* note.

> **"Love never dies a natural death. It dies because we don't know how to replenish its source. It dies of blindness and errors and betrayals. It dies of illness and wounds; it dies of weariness, of witherings, of tarnishings."**
>
> Anaïs Nin

#222 Get a Special Photo Framed

If you have a special photo of you and your loved one taken, get it enlarged and framed, then wrap it and give it as a present for no special reason or on a special occasion.

 ## #223 Create a "Best Of" Listing

Research the best accomplishments that occurred during each year of your time together as a couple. Include things like Grammy winning songs, Oscar winning films (in all categories), beauty contestant winners for local, state, beauty contests, local, state and presidential election winners, national, international, college and sports champions (e.g., Super bowl, NBA, golf, Olympics, or whatever interests your loved one). Present the list to your spouse or significant other on special anniversary dates (e.g., 5, 10, 15 years and so on). You can update the listing every five years and eventually turn it into a printed book for a milestone anniversary (e.g., 25, 50 or more).

 ## #224 Have Caricatures Drawn

When you go to a local festival, theme park or other location where caricature artists are present, have images of you and your loved one in humorous poses created. Frame the picture(s) to hang on your wall at home as a reminder of the excursion.

#225 Give a Hobby Gift Certificate

If your loved one has a hobby, buy a gift certificate to a store specializing in the equipment, tools and materials used for the hobby.

"When you stop expecting people to be perfect, you can like them for who they are."

Donald Miller

 **#226 Get an Autograph**

If your loved one has a favorite living author or musician, go to that artist's Website, find contact information and reach out to the person or group. Explain that your spouse or significant other is a fan and ask for an autographed photo, book, or album (you might have to purchase these on the Website). Most of these professionals are happy to provide autographed items.

 **#227 Order a Coin for Special Occasions**

The U.S. Mint and mints of other countries produce silver coins (e.g., dollar or equivalent) each year. Order one of these for each year of your relationship and present it as an anniversary or birthday present to your spouse or significant. On special anniversaries (e.g., 10th, 25th, and so on) you might splurge and order a gold coin. Check http://www.usmint.gov for details.

> "When we love, we always strive to become better than we are. When we strive to become better than we are, everything around us becomes better too."
> Paulo Coelho

 **#228 Create Customized Love Coupons**

Create a book of customized coupons to give to your spouse or significant other. These can be redeemed by you whenever your loved one chooses. Visit http://love-coups.com/ or search the Internet for other coupon book sources.

#229 Subscribe to a Favorite Publication

If your spouse or significant other has a hobby or enjoys a particular magazine, submit a one-year subscription order for him or her and give it as a gift certificate (you can print generic gift certificates off the Internet) in a greeting card. This might be for a special occasion or just to say *I Love You* as a surprise.

#230 Give a One-Year Club Membership

If your spouse or significant other likes to work out at a gym, play golf or tennis, or has other similar interests, provide him or her with a one-year subscription or extension of the current club or organization membership.

#231 Give a Copy of This Book

After reading through this book, give it to your loved one with your favorite parts highlighted. Maybe you will be getting some future surprises of your own.

> *"Absence diminishes mediocre passions and increases great ones as the wind extinguishes candles and flames fires."*
> Francois de La Rochefoucauld

MY PLAN FOR LOVE WORKSHEET

BUILDING AND MAINTAINING a loving, lasting relationship with another person is like having a successful garden; it takes continued effort and attention in order to succeed. You cannot just say I love you once and move on. Regular reinforcement of the sentiment and a true caring for your spouse or significant other are crucial.

Think about the strategies that you have read about in this book and techniques that you have used or seen others use in the past that send a powerful message of love and commitment to others. Jot down your own strategies here and plan to use these on a regular basis. You might do this by picking a sampling from this book or developing your own strategies.

_____

_____

_____

_____

_____

_____

_____

"If you love someone, you'll be willing to give up everything for them. But if they love you, they'll never ask you to."

Unknown

55 THINGS TO KNOW ABOUT YOUR LOVED ONE

MANY PEOPLE ARE surprised about how much they do not know about their spouse or significant other. To help build your relationship, provide a basis for discussion and help you better understand your loved one make sure that you each know the following favorites and least favorites for one another. To gain more in-depth understanding, each of you should identify your favorite and least favorite for each item below and tell "why" for each category.

1. Characteristic about you
2. Childhood memory
3. Memory since you became a couple
4. Memory before your relationship
5. Romantic memory with your loved one
6. Birthday
7. Subject in school
8. Subject in college
9. Color
10. Gemstone
11. Type of jewelry (e.g., yellow/white gold, silver, platinum)
12. Flower
13. Color hair
14. Color eyes

55 Things To Know About Your Loved One

15. Smell
16. Male cologne/after shave
17. Female perfume/cologne
18. Year/Make of car
19. Car color
20. Type of alcoholic drink
21. Type of non-alcoholic drink
22. Ethnic cuisine
23. Entrée
24. Vegetable
25. Candy
26. Snack food
27. Fruit
28. Dessert
29. Fast food
30. Restaurant
31. Time of day
32. Time of year
33. Holiday
34. City in your country
35. City in another country
36. Country
37. Leisure activity
38. Type of vacation
39. Vacation activity
40. Game

55 Things To Know About Your Loved One

41. Sport
42. Book genre (e.g., fiction, non-fiction, romance, biography, travel)
43. Book
44. Movie genre (e.g., suspense, horror, romance, documentary)
45. Movie
46. Actor
47. Actress
48. Type of music
49. Song
50. Singer
51. Type of pet
52. Historical period
53. Historical figure
54. Beautiful scenery ever experienced
55. Fun outdoor activity with your loved one

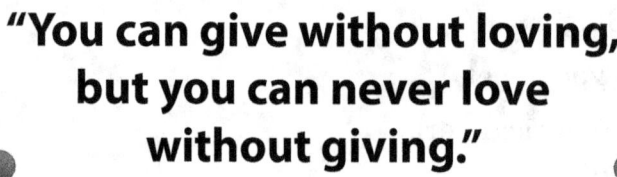

"You can give without loving, but you can never love without giving."

Unknown

RESOURCES FOR LOVERS

To find out more about these books or to order, follow the link provided for each title.

Books

131 Dirty Talk Examples: Learn How to Talk Dirty with The Simple Phrases That Drive Your Lover Wild and Beg You for Sex Tonight by Elizabeth Cramer. Go to http://amzn.to/1KKJjg5

131 Sex Games & Erotic Role Plays for Couples by Elizabeth Cramer. Go to http://amzn.to/1ML8P9v

1,000 Places to See in the United States and Canada before You Die by Pamela Schultz. Go to http://amzn.to/1JWv3GD

1,000 Places to See Before You Die by Patricia Schultz. Go to http://amzn.to/1JWv3GdD

4,000 Questions for Getting to Know Anyone and Everyone, 2nd Ed by Barbra Ann Kipler. Go to http://amzn.to/1MRF2xt

Bed & Breakfast and Country Inns by Deborah Edwards Sakach. Go to http://amzn.to/1JWwi8Y

Berlitz Cruising and Cruise Ships by Douglas Ward. Go to http://amzn.to/1hEzjyr

Berlitz River Cruising in Europe by Douglas Ward. Go to http://amzn.to/1hc71KM

Better Sex: AARP's Guide to Sex after 50 by Dr. Pepper Schwartz http://bit.ly/1O7O75A

Resources For Lovers

Couple Skills: Making Your Relationship Work by Matthew McKay PhD, Patrick Fanning, and Kim Paleg PhD. Go to http://amzn.to/1Id4EwY

Cruise Vacations for Dummies by Heidi Sarna and Hannafin. Go to http://amzn.to/1NShzJII

Dream Sleep: Castle & Palace Hotels in Europe by Pamela Burns. Go to http://amzn.to/1NShJRs

Getaway Guide to the Great Sex Weekend by Pepper Schwartz PhD and Janet Lever PhD. Go to http://amzn.to/1U4G65m

Getting the Love You Want: A Guide for Couples, 20th Anniversary Edition by Harville Hendrix. Go to http://amzn.to/1LvdESX

Loving Sex: The Book of Joy and Passion by Laura Berman. Go to http://amzn.to/1N2gwtz

Men, Women and Relationships: Making Peace with the Opposite Sex by John Gray. Go to http://amzn.to/1hc8Wih

Off the Beaten Path: A Travel Guide to More Than 1,000 Scenic and Interesting Places Still Uncrowded and Inviting by Reader's Digest. Go to http://amzn.to/1hZr6EH

Oral Sex She'll Never Forget: 50 Positions and Techniques That Will Make Her Like She Never Has Before by Dr. Sonia Borg. Go to http://amzn.to/1Id6xK1

Real Sex for Real Women: Intimacy, Pleasure and Sexual Well-Being by Laura Berman. Go to http://amzn.to/1hZrkvu

Sex and Marriage: How to Guide for Sex and Passion and Desire for Couples by Rochelle Foxx. Go to http://amzn.to/1Ubnj30

Resources For Lovers

Sex for Dummies by Dr. Ruth Westheimer and Pierre A. Lahu. Go to http://amzn.to/1PwMbRv

Stern's Guide to the Cruise Vacation by Steven B. Stern. Go to http://amzn.to/1hEARZd

Talk Dirty to Me: An Intimate Philosophy of Sex by Sallie Tisdale. Go to http://amzn.to/1fEaJf8

That's Not What I Meant!: How Conversational Style Makes or Breaks Relationships by Deborah Tannen. Go to http://amzn.to/1fEaMro

The Book of Massage: The Complete Guide to Eastern & Western Technique by Lucinda Lidell, Carola Beresford Cooke, and Anthony Porter. Go to http://amzn.to/1Ki2ulE

The Complete Guide to Bed & Breakfasts, Inns and Guesthouses International by Pamela Lanier. Go to http://amzn.to/1KKN9WC

The Cosmo Kama Sutra: 99 Mind-Blowing Sex Positions by the Editors of Cosmopolitan. Go to http://amzn.to/1JwTmcf

The Gender Communication Connection by Teri Gamble and Michael Gamble. Go to http://amzn.to/1Jhyp1w

The Joy of Sex: A Gourmet Guide to Love Making by Alex Comfort and Susan Quilliam. Go to http://amzn.to/1ETYTnE

The Lost Art of Listening: How Learning to Listen Can Improve Relationships by Michael P. Nichols. Go to http://amzn.to/1MLcS5M

The Massage Book by George Downing. Go to http://amzn.to/1V7Ix4k

The Modern Kama Sutra: The Ultimate Guide to the Secrets of Erotic Pleasure by Kamini Thomas and Kirk Thomas. Go to http://amzn.to/1NzzTKL

The Relationship Skills Workbook: A Do-It-Yourself Guide to a Thriving Relationship by Julia B. Colwell PhD. Go to http://amzn.to/1MRIic8

Ultimate G-Spot Orgasm & Ejaculation Secrets: Give Her Mind-Blowing Pleasure by Safe Sex Initiative. Go to http://amzn.to/1PwN50i

What Men Really Want in Bed: The Surprising Secrets Men Wish Women Knew About Sex by Cynthia W. Gentry. Go to http://amzn.to/1Ei395H

What Women Really Want in Bed: The Surprising Secrets Women Wish Men Knew About Sex by Cynthia W. Gentry and Dana Fredsti. Go to http://amzn.to/1JWG7Up

You Just Don't Understand: Men and Women in Conversation by Deborah Tannen. Go to http://amzn.to/1LyvY05

Instructional Videos/Toys/Games/Clothing

Better Sex http://bit.ly/1XXmNup

Eve's Garden http://bit.ly/1FxN6M6

Frederick's of Hollywood http://bit.ly/1JTv7lp

Sinclair Institute http://bit.ly/1O13FYP

Victoria's Secret http://bit.ly/1UBte73

Romantic/Sensuous/Sexy/Erotic Movies

9 ½ Weeks

Basic Instinct

Body Double

Body Heat

Chloe

Emmanuelle

Henry and June

Last Tango in Paris

Love Affair

Secretary

Sliver

The Lover

The Piano

The Story of O

Titanic

Wild Orchid

Travel Magazines

Afar http://www.afar.com/

Conde Nast Traveler http://www.cntraveler.com/

Cosmo http://www.cosmopolitan.com

Islands http://www.islands.com/

National Geographic http://www.nationalgeographic.com

National Geographic Travel http://on.natgeo.com/1JDWizj

National Parks http://bit.ly/1MUNZod

Trailer Life http://bit.ly/1LK1JUi

Travel 50 & Beyond http://bit.ly/1Esmkdb

Travel + Leisure http://tandl.me/1F7Ia0h

Vacations http://bit.ly/1Q0k8Lf

Cruise Lines/Travel Agents

AMA Waterways (River cruises) http://www.amawaterways.com

American Cruise Lines (U.S. river cruises) http://www.americancruiselines.com

Avalon Waterways (River cruises) http://www.avalonwaterways.com

Bahamas Paradise Cruise Line http://www.bahamsparadisecruise.com

Carnival Cruise Lines http://www.carnival.com

Celebrity Cruises http://www.celebritycruises.com

Costa Cruise Lines http://www.costacruise.com

CroisieEurope River Cruises http://www.croisieuporerivercruises.com/

Crystal Cruises http://www.crystalcruises.com

Cunard Cruise Lines http://www.cunard.com

Disney Cruise Lines http://www.disneycruise.disney.go.com

Haimark Lines (Great Lakes, Caribbean, Central & S. America) http://www.haimarkline.com

Holland America Cruise Lines http://www.hollandamerica.com

Norwegian Cruises http://www.ncl.com

Pearl Seas Cruises http://www.peralseascruises.com

Princess Cruise Lines http://www.princess.com

Regent Seven Seas Cruises http://www.rssc.com

Royal Caribbean Cruise http://www.royalcaribbean.com

Seabourn Cruise Lines http://www.seabourn.com

Resources For Lovers

Silversea Cruises http://www.silversea.com

TBSTravel http://ourcruiseagent.com/ 877-492-1201

Uniworld Boutique River Cruises http://www.uniworld.com/

Vantage Cruise Line (International river cruises) http://vantagetravel/com/cruises

Viking River Cruises http://www.vikingriver-cruises.com

Windstar Luxury Cruises http://www.windstarcruises.com

"Carpe diem (Seize the day).

Horace

ABOUT THE AUTHOR

THROUGHOUT HIS LIFE Bob Lucas has considered himself a romantic and has been a student of human nature and has researched and written articles and books on interpersonal relationship skills. He has trained thousands of people on how to more effectively, listen, read nonverbal cues, project a positive self-image and better understand the behaviors of others. He incorporates that expertise and experience in this book.

As an internationally-known award-winning author, independent publisher, learning and performance expert Bob specializes in workplace performance-based training and consulting services and is Principal of *Robert W. Lucas Enterprises*. He has over four decades of experience in human resources development, management, and customer service in a variety of organizational environments. Bob has served on various non-profit boards where he has been President of the Central Florida Chapter of the Association for Talent Development (formerly the American Society for Training and Development), Chair of Leadership Seminole in Seminole County, Florida and on the board for the Florida Authors and Publishers Association (FAPA).

Bob is also an avid writer. He has the top selling customer service textbook in the United States and has written and contributed to thirty-seven books and hundreds of training leader guides, and support materials for several training videos.

About The Author

Bob earned a Bachelor of Science degree in Law Enforcement from the University of Maryland, an M.A degree with a focus in Human Resources Development from George Mason University in Fairfax, Virginia, and a second M.A. degree in Management and Leadership from Webster University in Orlando, Florida.

CONTACT BOB LUCAS:

Phone: +1-407-695-5535 (United States)

E-Mail: info@robertwlucas.com

Website: http://www.robertwlucas.com

Like Bob at:
http://www.facebook.com/robertwlucasenterprises

Non-Fiction Writing Blog:
http://www.robertwlucas.com/wordpress

Creative Training Blog:
http://www.thecreativetrainer.com

Customer Service Blog:
http://customerserviceskillsbook.com

BOOKS BY ROBERT W. LUCAS

All of the following books are available at your local book retailer and at www.robertwlucas.com.

Make Money Writing Books: Proven Profit-Making Strategies for Authors

Please Every Customer: Delivering Stellar Customer Service across Cultures

Energize Your Training: Creative Techniques to Engage Learners

Customer Service Skills for Success

Training Workshop Essentials: Designing, Developing and Delivering Learning Events That Get Results

Creative Learning: Activities and Games That REALLY Engage People

The Creative Training Idea Book: Inspired Tips & Techniques for Engaging and Effective Learning

The BIG Book of Flip Charts

How to be a Great Call Center Representative

"Thoughts become feelings, feelings become love, and love comes from the heart."

Erich Fromm

ABOUT ROBERT W. LUCAS ENTERPRISES

ROBERT W. LUCAS ENTERPRISES is the parent company for Success Skills Press (publisher of this book). In addition, it is an organization dedicated to providing "real world" training and performance solutions to organizations and individuals. Bob Lucas, Principal of the organization, works closely with a network of strategic partners to help clients assess organizational, environmental, and individual human resources needs and challenges. Bob then helps develop or provide appropriate customized strategies and solutions to address identified needs and challenges.

Bob and his associates are highly skilled and knowledgeable professionals who have a wide range of experience in large organizational settings. They are uniquely qualified to provide human resource consultative services and training interventions and stand ready to help provide customized solutions to meet client requirements.

Some of the specialized training topics offered include:

- *Interpersonal Communication (verbal, non-verbal, and listening skills)*
- *Coaching Skills*
- *Train-the-Trainer and Presentation Skills*
- *Customer Service Skills and Interventions*
- *Teambuilding*
- *Management/Supervisory Skills*

About Robert W. Lucas Enterprises

For additional information on Robert W. Lucas Enterprises call (407) 695-5535 or visit http://www.robertwlucas.com.

Visit http://www.robertwlucas.com for free articles and additional resources.

REQUEST FOR REVIEWS

FEED BACK IS IMPORTANT in your relationship. It is also important to an author. Likewise, I will appreciate your visiting Amazon (http://amazon.com) and leaving some objective feedback about this book. Your comments will also aid other potential readers in making a decision on whether to purchase a copy of this book.

I have a passion for what I do and hope that comes across in my writing. My goal in writing this book, and others, is to provide you with information and ideas that can enhance your potential for success in life and build stronger relationships with those you love. I hope that the content of this book prompted some thoughts on your part and that you will put some real effort into developing and solidifying your interpersonal relationships in the future.

If you have specific suggestions related to the content or format of the book, please email your thoughts to me at info@robertwlucas.com with a subject line of *"Feedback on 101 Ways to Say I Love You."* Provide me a name and complete mailing address in the text area and I will send you a copy of the first edition of my booklet *Communicating One-To-One: Making the Most of Interpersonal Relationships.*

Thanks for your assistance. If you would like to be added to a mailing list to learn about my other books and ones that I will be publishing in the future, please email me at info@robertwlucas.com with a subject line of "Add to Mailing List."

Request For Reviews

In order to stay in touch and up-to-date on new products and services that I offer from time-to-time, please remember to visit my blogs via www.robertwlucas.com and to Like me on Facebook at https://www.facebook.com/robertwlucasbookauthor.

Let me know if I can be of future assistance.

Thank you.
Bob Lucas

ORDER FORM
231 WAYS TO SAY I LOVE YOU

Cost USD	Quantity	Sub-Total
1 copy @ $12.95 each		
2-10 @ $11.65 each		
11-50 @ $10.35 each		
51+ @ $ 9.05 each		
Recipients in Florida add applicable:		
State and local taxes		
Shipping/Handling		
TOTAL		

Shipping/Handling: 1 copy =$3.95   2-6 copies= $5.95

7 or more and international = based on weight (call/email before ordering)

Overnight Express and international delivery available at actual cost, plus $5.00.

☐ **Check here for express delivery**

NOTE: Prices subject to change without notice.

Checks drawn on U.S. Banks in U.S. currency only and U.S. Postal Money Orders accepted.

Check/MO# _____ enclosed

Ship To Address (No P.O. Boxes please):

_____

_____

Phone:

Email:

Mail To:

Robert W. Lucas Enterprises
**1555 Pinehurst Drive
Casselberry, FL 32707
USA**

PH:+1-(407)695-5535

Email : info@robertwlucas.com